justinguitar.com
Beginner's Course

justinguitar.com
Beginner's Course

Justin Sandercoe

Wise Publications
part of The Music Sales Group
London / New York / Paris / Sydney / Copenhagen / Berlin / Madrid / Hong Kong / Tokyo

Published by
Wise Publications
14-15 Berners Street, London W1T 3LJ, UK.

Exclusive Distributors:
Music Sales Limited
Distribution Centre, Newmarket Road,
Bury St Edmunds, Suffolk IP33 3YB, UK.

Music Sales Pty Limited
Units 3-4, 17 Willfox Street, Condell Park, NSW 2200, Australia.

Order No. AM1001440R
ISBN: 978-1-78305-892-1
This book © Copyright 2011 Wise Publications, a division of Music Sales Limited.

Written by Justin Sandercoe.
Edited by Tom Farncombe.
Design by Fresh Lemon.
Photography by Matthew Ward.
Cover design by Paul Agar.
Cover photographs by Nick Delaney.
CD recorded by Justin Sandercoe.
CD mastered by Jonas Persson.
Printed in the EU

www.musicsales.com

www.justinguitar.com

Justin Sandercoe is a London-based guitarist, songwriter, performer, producer and educator who grew up in Tasmania. He has been based in West London since 1996.

As well as teaching many thousands of students online, over the last 20 years Justin has been a tutor at The Guitar Institute (the ICMP) and taught hundreds of private students, of all ages and abilities, in many styles. His celebrity students have included Katie Melua and Cathy Dennis.

Justinguitar.com first went live in July 2003 as a small website offering a few lessons as a sample to promote private lessons. It grew steadily over its first few years, with Justin often adding content to keep himself occupied while on tour, much of it done on a laptop in hotel rooms around the globe.

After seeing the popularity of YouTube, Justin began making instructional guitar videos in December 2006, initially filmed and edited by his friend Jed Wardley. By September 2011 his YouTube instructional videos had been watched over 100,000,000 (yep, that's 100 million) times and the website receives well over 20,000 unique visitors a day.

The site has received many accolades in both the traditional and new media. By keeping quality guitar instruction free for those that cannot afford private lessons he has given the site a huge user base right around the world, helping the poor, the shy and those who are simply too busy to make regular lessons.

His approach promotes patience; learning each thing really well, and being able to use it before you move on to learn more. The method works, and hundreds of thousands of people around the world have benefited from the lessons on the site.

As the The Independent newspaper says, he is "One of the most influential guitar teachers in history".

Contents

Before we start learning chords and stuff, I want to get you off to the best possible start. This section will really help you get the most out of this course, so check it out!

In this first stage we are going to check out three basic chords, how to change between them, and the very basics of rhythm.

Now we are going to introduce some easy minor chords. We'll be changing between them and listening to the difference between major and minor. We'll also develop the changes between the new chords and the ones learnt in the previous lesson. We also get our feet tapping and understand why it is important to become friends with a metronome.

Now we have to get your hand stretching to play a couple of trickier chords. We also introduce the idea of strumming patterns and learn how to play the simplest of rhythms.

Now we are going to introduce some more interesting (but not necessarily harder-to-play) chords. We introduce the 'partial barre' to toughen up the side of your 1st finger a bit and also talk about counting rhythms; all important stuff.

In this stage we finish off learning our open 7th chords, check out a new way to get your chord changes even faster and also have a look at shuffle rhythms. You will be able to play a blues in three different keys by the end of this stage! We'll also have a little look at some basic music theory knowledge.

Stage 6 — 106

OK. This is a big stage: lots of important stuff. It's time to tackle the big, nasty F Chord. Get ready for a bit of pain and frustration! Everyone has to go through this rite of passage. And that is not all—we also have to learn to miss some strums! This is harder than it sounds... but it is lots of fun and will sound awesome once you get it!

Stage 7 — 120

Now you have the basics under your fingers, we can start to look at some more interesting stuff—notes on the neck, some cool chords to spice up your playing and your first scale!

Stage 8 — 140

Now we are ready for some really cool stuff: a look at some other common ways of playing the G Chord, a 12-Bar Blues and an exercise to help you get your picking skills a bit sharper.

Stage 9 — 158

Now we are nearly at the end of our beginner's course. Just a few more things to learn, and then it's consolidation time! There is a whole lot of different material here, so just try and digest one little bit at a time.

Bonus Stage — 176

In this bonus stage we've included some useful reference charts, a further J.U.S.T.I.N. method training exercise and some fun things to play on your own: a solo blues song, a fingerstyle version of Silent Night and an easy blues lead thang to play along with a backing track!

Welcome to my beginner's guitar course!

This course starts at the very beginning, giving you advice about the first steps that you need to take—like buying an instrument—and what to expect on the fun and rewarding (and sometimes frustrating!) journey that is learning to play the guitar. I know this course works, because I have developed it over 20 years by teaching hundreds of students of all ages and abilities, and I aim to start you off on a really well-structured, enjoyable and motivating course that will have you playing real songs in as short a time as possible.

There are, of course, many different ways to learn the guitar, but I'd like to think that my course is the most effective method available anywhere. It has been carefully refined in response to user questions and comments on my website forum. Well over 50,000 people have used this course already, and there have been many small improvements made to it since its launch in June 2009.

How to use this course

If you've played a bit before, you can adapt this course to fit your prior knowledge, picking out lessons as you want them. However, I would advise that you read the whole method from the beginning, even if you are already familiar with some of the topics covered. By reading through all the lessons, you may well find a few little nuggets of knowledge that help put it all together.

The J.U.S.T.I.N. Method (Just Use Sound To Improve Now)

So what makes this course special? The J.U.S.T.I.N. method! I managed to use my name to make a silly acronym to define my own method (my middle name is megalomaniac!). Learning to use your ears in the early stages of learning to play guitar is the thing that I believe will make you a much better player than any other teaching method I have ever seen. It develops the skills you need to transcribe guitar music. This is something that is missing from most methods, but is the way that all the great guitarists of previous generations got so good, and why so many guitarists these days are not as popular or inspiring as the great players of previous generations.

The J.U.S.T.I.N. training exercises are audio, and so you'll have to listen to the CDs to use them (they're online as well). Remember, music is about listening, and not about reading. Skip over them and you will be missing a very important piece of the puzzle that you will most likely regret later.

Songs

Learning songs is an important part of this method. My advice is to go through the course and learn as many songs as you can. The perfect partner to the course is the Justinguitar.com Beginner's Songbook which has songs to match each stage (Order No. AM1001429). Also, work on the J.U.S.T.I.N. method to help train your ears. Then, at the end of this course, you should start transcribing as much material as you can. You can also buy official tab songbooks, which will have been transcribed by professionals and should be accurate, but be very careful of using free tabs on the internet; many of them are completely wrong. Whatever you do, make sure you use your ears to check what is right.

Practical Music Theory

Although learning about music theory is not an essential part of learning to play the guitar, many people want to understand what they are doing. My eBook, Practical Music Theory (PMT—available to purchase from my website), will be very interesting for those people and will give you lots of exercises to help you memorise the information. Music theory goes way beyond the few concepts taught in this course, so check PMT out.

Any Questions?

If you have any questions the best place to ask is the forum (www.justinguitarcommunity. com), where you'll find help from me and many other experienced players. Try and leave your lessons in the right topic so they will get answered. Silly or inappropriate questions just get deleted straightaway! Once a question has been incorporated in the main text it is also deleted.

Posting a question in the forum also helps me update the course and to answer other people's questions before they even have them!

Good luck. I'm sure you'll have a lot of fun learning the guitar with me!

Justin Sandercoe
November 2011, London

Getting Started

Stage 1
Stage 2
Stage 3
Stage 4
Stage 5
Stage 6
Stage 7
Stage 8
Stage 9
Bonus

 ## Introduction

Let's get started by looking at some of the most common questions I get asked about learning the guitar. The guitar is an easy instrument to play badly, but with practice anyone can learn to play well. In this lesson I just want to clear up a few things so that you know what to expect of this course, and of yourself.

Am I too old to start learning?

I find it amusing that I get this question a lot… from 16 year olds! You are never too old to start playing and enjoying guitar. Sure, you will read about the guitar legends we all admire, and how they started when they were six months old and were playing the Albert Hall by the time they were two, but that's not the case for most guitarists.

It seems that about a quarter of the people using my website are over 50 years old and loving it. It's a wonderful hobby and I have had a few students in their 50s that started gigging regularly after a few years practice; a couple even turned professional! So it is never too late.

One thing to be aware of however is that children do tend to learn faster than adults. I've been surprised time and time again at how quickly children between 12–18 learn stuff. I guess because they are still growing they develop the muscles in their hands faster, but they also have less pre-conceived ideas about what might be difficult to learn. Many grown-ups will hear a song and think "that sounds amazing, I bet it's very hard to play" and struggle if they try, whereas an 18 year old will hear the same thing and think "that sounds amazing, I want to learn that" and then do it without thinking about how hard it might be.

Just remember it's mostly about practice time: put in a lot of time and you'll get good, no matter what your age!

How quickly will I be able to play songs?

You should be able to play a basic song or two after about three to five hours of practice (over a week or more—not in one go). It probably won't sound perfect, but it will at least be recognizable. How much time it takes you to learn the basics will depend almost totally on how much you practise. Note that if I give a recommended practice time— say, five minutes—it means five minutes of intense practice, not half-watching TV or answering phone calls or whatever. Try to stay focused when you practise, and don't let yourself drift off into random jamming or playing that old favourite…again!

How often do I need to practise?

If you play for fifteen minutes a week, expect it to take at least a year to get the very basics under your fingers. However, if you practise for fifteen minutes a day, you will notice that things are getting easier after just one week. There is such a thing as 'natural aptitude'—so some people naturally learn things faster than others—but perseverance will always prevail. Lots of people who learn slowly at first learn better and faster in the long run (usually because those people are taking the time to figure out why they are doing what).

Do I have to practise every day?

Yes! The best way (and I do know this is not always possible) is to try and find a little time to practise every day. It is much better to do 10 minutes a day, 7 days a week, than one hour of practice every Saturday; aim for daily practice. If this isn't possible, at least try to get in a little time regularly and then have one main practice time each week. Many of my students have found that playing at the same time (such as straight after dinner, or when you first get home after work/ school, or just before you go to bed) is the best way to develop a consistent routine. There's more advice on practising on page 20.

Do I have to follow your suggested practice routine?

Well, I'm suggesting it for a reason, and that is that most people need to work on similar things. However, everyone is different, and so if you feel the routine does not fit well for you, then change it. But try and keep to the general structure: it works!

My fingers hurt and have deep grooves in them, should I stop practising?

Yes, if it is painful at all, then you should take a break. It's normal for things to be a little sore at the beginning. Getting grooves in your fingers is quite normal, and they are just from the strings sitting in the same place under your fingers (which is good). They will toughen up after a short time and then

Getting Started

Stage 1

Stage 2

Stage 3

Stage 4

Stage 5

Stage 6

Stage 7

Stage 8

Stage 9

Bonus

you won't notice it at all. The very first few times you play your fingertips are likely to get VERY sore in a very quickly (in 5 minutes or even less!) but don't worry: just put the guitar down for a while and come back to it later. It's normal. Sometimes the lines in your fingers can stay there for a whole day after you finish. Don't worry about this! Some people like to start playing on a nylon string guitar when they're starting out, for this very reason. It hurts a little less I guess, but it shouldn't be long before your fingers toughen up enough to play for 10 or 15 minutes on a steel string guitar without crying! Try not to let it get to the point of a blister, because then you need to take a few days off to let it heal. Also, make sure your hands are dry when you play; if you practise right after a shower or after doing the washing up then the skin will last hardly any time at all.

If you get any pain in your hand or forearm you should stop straight away and see a doctor if the pain persists. Playing should be fun and enjoyable, not painful.

What strings should I use?

If you are beginner playing steel string acoustic or electric guitar you probably want to start with very thin strings. On electric they are referred to as '9s' (.09 to .46 inches thick); on acoustic you would use '11s' (.11 to .52 inches thick). If you just go to a shop and ask for light strings—or 9s or 11s—you should be given the right set. However, this is really a matter of personal preference. Some people prefer thicker strings, and don't mind the pain so much. Thicker strings tend to have a fatter sound too, which many people prefer. I use 11s on electric and 13s on acoustics.

The string thickness (or string gauge) is a lot less important with nylon strings, so any set will do. There's more about strings on page 16.

I only want to play rock guitar (or country guitar or jazz or whatever): why do I have to play pop songs and rhythm guitar?

What you should learn when you first start—no matter what style you want to aspire to—is the same basic chords, and developing a sense of rhythm. Any serious guitarist in any style should know all of the things in this course. Often learning things in one style will help your playing in many other styles. Even if you might think that a particular skill is not needed for what you want to do, you will often miss an important technique or a 'piece of the puzzle' that you will be searching for later!

My advice is to follow the course all the way through and then decide what things you might want to specialize in.

We don't learn much about rhythm in the first few stages. Why?

Learning to play good and consistent rhythm guitar is only possible when your strumming hand can move without stopping. This helps you get in the groove and keeps your timing solid. If you can't change chords fast enough, then you will keep putting little stops in your strumming and this is a very bad thing to learn. If you work on building up the speed of your chord changes first, you will start playing rhythm easily. People learn a lot faster this way: by mastering the individual elements first and then combining them.

Do I need to grow my fingernails?

It is very important that the fingernails on your fretting hand (the one that holds down the notes on the neck) are very short or they will make your hand go in a funny position. I have fake nails on my strumming hand because I play guitar a lot, and natural nails just don't last long enough. They can help with fingerstyle playing but many great players use flesh and not nails, so you don't have to have fake fingernails. In fact, I don't recommend getting fake (acrylic) nails unless you want people giving you funny looks when you go out! See more on this on page 147.

Does it matter if I'm left-handed?

No! Many lefties play right-handed, but you can buy a left-handed guitar, or string a right-hander upside down (like Jimi Hendrix). There's advice on the forum about being a left-handed player. In this book we've tried to use 'fretting hand' and 'strumming hand' to avoid dictating which hand you're using.

The Justinguitar.com Forum

Please use the forum on the website if you have any questions not covered here. I would love to help you all individually but I just don't have that much time. I go there as often as I can and help out, but there are many experienced players there too that help out a lot. So if you have any questions, please check there first!

Getting Started

Stage 1

Stage 2

Stage 3

Stage 4

Stage 5

Stage 6

Stage 7

Stage 8

Stage 9

Bonus

Electric or acoustic?

One of the most frequently asked questions from beginner players is whether to choose electric or acoustic. The advice here is my view. Others may disagree, and they are welcome to their opinion; mine is subject to change without notice!

The big beginner's debate

The basic types of guitar are:

- Electric (including hollow-bodied or semi-acoustics) (PICTURE 1)
- Acoustic (steel stringed — including those with electrics fitted, otherwise called electro-acoustics) (PICTURE 2)
- Classical (nylon stringed) (PICTURE 3)

Note that 'semi-acoustics' are not really acoustic— they are electric guitars with a semi-hollow body, and so are sometimes confusingly referred to as semi-acoustics. However, they play like electrics.

Also note that electro-acoustics are not electric guitars. They are acoustic instruments with electronics fitted so that they can be amplified, but you would not normally need to plug them in to get a good sound out of them.

Many people think that electric guitars are going to be loud when they are plugged in... well, they do have a volume control, so you can control the volume. Also, be aware that you do not have to plug them in! I do probably half of my practice on electric guitar without any amp at all. It's good to get the notes ringing out loud and clear without an amp, so as a beginner you might want to put all your money into getting a cool guitar and leave getting an amp until later.

So lets look at the pros and cons of each type of guitar and the factors to consider when choosing between them.

Playability

Electric guitars are generally the easiest to play: the strings are thinner, the 'action' is low (see below) and therefore they are easier to press down. Barre chords on acoustic guitar can be very demanding and require a lot of finger strength. Cheaper acoustic guitars can be very hard to play higher up the fretboard. Classical guitars have nylon strings, which are softer than steel strings, and easier to press down. However, the neck is much wider on a classical guitar, which can be a struggle for

beginners. The action is likely to be higher, as well. In general, they are softer-toned and don't project as well as a steel string acoustic, which makes for quieter practising, which could be a consideration.

Action

The distance from the strings to the neck is called the action. When it is very low it is easy to press the strings down; when it is too low the strings will buzz when you play. If a guitar's action is too high it will be very hard to play, and for a beginner this can be pretty disheartening.

I recommend that you get a guitar with a low action so that it can be played easily. The small tonal benefits of having a higher action can be dealt with in a few years when it becomes important. At the start what is important is enjoying playing!

Getting your guitar action set up by a good luthier can make a huge difference to your guitar's playability (you'll usually find someone at your local store). I have a number of private students that found an AMAZING difference when they had set their guitar up correctly, and of course I get all mine done too. If you are struggling to play barre chords on an acoustic guitar, then a too-high action could certainly be a part of the problem.

Sound And Style

Deciding which instrument to start with can be pretty simple if you think in terms of style!

- If you want to play rock, get an electric.
- If you want to play folk or fingerstyle, a steel string acoustic is the best choice.
- If you want to play classical then you need a nylon string classical guitar.

It all depends on what style you want to play. If you like death metal you probably don't want to buy a pink Telecaster... think about what you like and what you are going to play!

If you want to play all styles, my advice is to go with an electric, and get an acoustic later.

justinguitar.com

Getting Started

Stage 1
Stage 2
Stage 3
Stage 4
Stage 5
Stage 6
Stage 7
Stage 8
Stage 9
Bonus

1.

2.

3.

Budget Acoustics Usually Suck

Very cheap acoustics are usually not such a great idea. Often their sound quality is poor and they are hard to play. I often see students selling them after a six-month struggle (if they managed to stick with it that long!). So if your budget is very tight, I would not get an acoustic. You may think you save a little because you don't need to buy an amplifier as well, but as I said before you don't have to use an amplifier to practise anyway.

After some internet searches I've found some acoustic packs (with a strap and picks) for less than £100/$175, and you can be pretty sure that these are not going to play well. People just can't make guitars that are easy to play at that price. If that is really your budget, then please spend it on a decent electric (and leave the amp for now).

Do I really need an amplifier?

Electric guitars need an amplifier to be heard above a singing voice, although they make enough sound just for practice instrumentally. There are also a number of units (like the Line 6 Pod and similar) that can be plugged into your stereo or computer, but this isn't much use if you want to play in a band. I did the majority of my practice on an electric guitar without an amplifier, and I think this helps you work on your tone, because you have to draw the volume out of the instrument. Having a good amp can help you sound like your favourite players—which is cool—but not so important when you are just starting out.

O.K., so which amplifier?

If you do want an amplifier, there is a vast array of models available with all kinds of fancy stuff built in—effects, digital modelling, even backing tracks! It really depends on your budget. It's very likely that a new amplifier will be your first major purchase if you stick with it (they make a bigger difference to your sound than the guitar does, believe it or not!) so my advice is to start small and simple, learn a bit, see where it is taking you and you will have a better idea of what to spend your hard-earned cash on. There's more about amps on page 182

Small Guitars

I often hear from people wondering if they should buy a 3/4-size guitar because their hands are small. My answer is simple: no!

3/4 guitars are fine for children under the age of 11, or as travel guitars, but if you want to learn properly, then buy a full size guitar at the start. I started on a full size classical guitar right back when I was knee high to a grasshopper; initally it's hard, but your fingers adapt fast enough and you will soon develop flexibility and dexterity. For children under 11, a 3/4 guitar is an option, but even then I still feel that full-size is better. Check out all the amazing 6 year-old kids playing amazing stuff on the internet—9 times out of 10 they are playing full-size instruments.

Stage 1
Stage 2
Stage 3
Stage 4
Stage 5
Stage 6
Stage 7
Stage 8
Stage 9
Bonus

 The verdict:

I think for the general beginner an electric guitar is probably the best instrument, mainly because they are a little easier to play and so you will see results faster, which will inspire you to play more. Here is my way of thinking about it:

- If you want to play rock: buy an electric.
- If you want to play classical: buy a nylon string classical guitar.
- If you want to play folk: buy a steel string acoustic.
- However, if you only have a very small budget, don't buy an acoustic.
- If you are not really sure, get an electric.
- Avoid a 3/4-size guitar unless it's for very young children.

So, my general recommendation is: buy a medium-priced electric guitar.

£200/$350 should get you a basic electric guitar, a few picks, a strap, a cheap tuner and a cable, if you shop around. Don't be afraid to go second-hand! I very rarely buy new instruments.

So which one then?

This is really just about personal choice. Everyone likes different guitars, but here are some of my thoughts on certain brands...

Steel String Acoustic

All my acoustics are made by an Australian company called Maton, and I think they are absolutely wonderful! They do a good range of guitars aiming from mid-price to high-end guitars, but they don't really do any starter priced guitars. If you have the budget for one (they start at around £600/$1000), they are awesome and will last you a long time!

I really don't think you should spend less than about £250 ($400) because you will end up with something hard to play, and you probably won't enjoy playing! At the cheaper end, both Yamaha and Fender make very good budget acoustic guitars. Lately I have played a lot of cheap Yamahas that were good; they are mass-produced, but mass-produced well.

Avoid the thin acoustics that look like electrics. They usually don't sound good either acoustically or plugged in. This includes Fender's 'Telecoustic' (I otherwise recommend Fender). I'm not really a big fan of any guitars made of anything other than wood either—none of that carbon stuff—just keep it simple.

Don't forget to check the action. If it's too high you will really struggle when it comes to barre chords and power chords later on. Make sure you have a play of it and make sure it feels comfortable for you.

At the higher end I rate Maton, Martin, Taylor and Guild, but once you are spending a couple of thousand, you should know what you want and what you need. Old guitars often sound great and have more character, which is something I don't really understand. Something must happen to the wood as the instrument gets older, as it seems that generally, old guitars sound best.

Electric

My favourite adage applies: buy cheap, buy twice. I rate the Yamaha Pacifica guitars (which start around £200/$350). They have a thin neck (which is good for rock) and consistently excellent build quality. I don't think there is much of a question about the quality of these guitars and most of the other teachers I respect recommend them as well. There are many cheaper guitars out there but for the few pounds you will save you are much better off going for a Pacifica in my humble opinion. I never owned one myself (and I don't have any kind of deal going with them at all), but have played many that students brought in over the years, which is why I recommend them to you!

Other good electric starters are the Epiphone SG; I have also been hearing very good things about the Vintage brand of guitars. I have played a few that belonged to students and they do seem good value. Also, there are some cheaper Ibanez guitars that sound great. Fender Squires are not bad either, though I've seen some badly set up ones with really cheap fittings, so be careful. Buying a proper USA-built Fender Stratocaster will always be awesome though if you have the budget!

Don't buy an electric with a floating tremolo when you start out.

If you are a beginner then you probably don't know what a 'floating tremolo' is. Have a look at Floyd Rose (www.floydrose.com), who made the first models. If you are looking at a guitar that has little tuners on the bridge, then it's probably a floating tremolo. For a beginner they are a total pain in the butt. They are very hard to tune and a real pain to change strings. The cheaper ones go out of tune a lot too. If you know why you want one, then fine, but locking tremolos on budget instruments are usually rubbish, so stay clear of those for now!

Classical

I think the Yamaha brand are excellent, and that's what I started on! There are many others of course but Yamaha consistently deliver a top notch product at a budget price.

If you are loaded, then just go and try one of the many beautiful handmade guitars available. I personally would like an old Ramirez guitar, but they cost as much as nice cars… maybe one day!

I've got GAS…

I swear if we all spent as much time practising as we do deciding which guitar to buy there would be a lot more great guitar players in the world. Seriously, dudes and dudettes, when you are starting out, just get yourself a guitar that plays well. If you dig playing guitar and play for a few years you are almost certainly going to want another guitar, even if your first guitar was awesome. It's called G.A.S. (Guitar Acquisition Syndrome) and it's a very painful condition for the wallet… I've been suffering for many years so now I'm just used to it!

Buying guitars is fun, and searching for the right one is fun too, but make sure you are actually doing enough practice as well, so you can enjoy your new toy when you get it!

Use The Forum

On the forum there are thousands of people at all stages of playing that can offer advice on new beginner guitars. I have to admit that I play only top-end gear and don't know the latest on all the new budget guitars, but on the forum there are people learning that can all give you advice based on personal experience, and there's no substitute for that!

There are even boards now for each specific instrument, so it's easy to get the advice you need. They are not solely aimed at beginners, but there is lots of advice from experienced players and I'm sure you'll get plenty of advice here from other GAS sufferers.

I can't actually tell you what guitar you should buy, so please don't email me to ask. All I can offer is the advice above, and my list of recommended products for beginners.

Getting Started
Stage 1
Stage 2
Stage 3
Stage 4
Stage 5
Stage 6
Stage 7
Stage 8
Stage 9
Bonus

Getting Started

Stage 1
Stage 2
Stage 3
Stage 4
Stage 5
Stage 6
Stage 7
Stage 8
Stage 9
Bonus

Introduction

There are some guitar accessories that you are definitely going to need quite soon, and some optional things that simply make your life a little easier. In this lesson I want to give you a little bit of advice regarding all these things. It is recommended that you sort these out at some point but you don't need to get them all before you start—all you really need is a guitar and some picks. There's more about picks on page 26.

Essential Shopping List

There are some things that are pretty much essential that you want to get before you think about starting out on the course, whether you're playing electric or acoustic.

Tuner

It is essential to get your guitar in tune! You should learn to tune up yourself, without needing a tuner, but when you are starting out, it is better to be in tune—and having your guitar sound nice—than trying to learn how to tune, messing it up, and having your guitar sound horrible. Have mercy on those that will listen to you learning and buy yourself a tuner right away!

Justin Recommends: Korg GA-1, or the Peterson iStrobosoft iPhone app.

Spare strings

Don't make the mistake of not having spare strings. Order some next time you buy any other stuff, and have at least two spare sets at home. Although 'treated' 'Extra Life' strings are a little more expensive, they don't rust and are better for people who don't change their strings very often; they keep sounding better for longer and are less likely to break.
You can use whatever strings you like. I like DR strings, but have played many brands over the years and there is not a whole lot in it. Many of my students like Elixir strings which last a long time.

There is advice on changing strings in the bonus section at the back of the book.

Justin Recommends: DR Extra-life Strings (I endorse DR, because I think they are awesome).

Strap

Getting a strap is a very good idea. It helps keep the guitar stable and trains you up for when you want to go unleash your skills on the world. Don't worry too much about what type to get—just one that you like. If you bought a heavy guitar (like a Gibson Les Paul) you might want to get a padded strap so you don't hurt your shoulder!

Justin Recommends: Any Strap!

Strap Locks

If you plan to stand up and use a strap on your guitar, then please buy some strap locks. These can range from plastic discs that cost very little, to big metal catches that you fix to your strap, which cost more. I have seen too many beginners without strap locks and seen guitars drop to the floor. I have actually seen three guitars snap necks because the strap fell off. The cheap ones work, so there is no excuse not to have these. You can also use the red rubber ring that is on the top of bottles of Grolsch Beer (the imported one with the 'pop top').Put it on the strap pin after you put the strap on. It's not quite as good as a proper strap lock, but has the added bonus of giving you a beer!

Justin Recommends: Schaller Strap Locks (around £20/$35) or Jim Dunlop Lok Strap (about £3/$5)

16

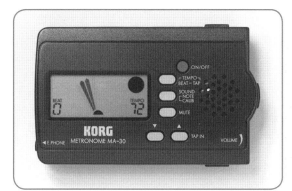

Metronome

This one is important. You will use your metronome a lot. Any metronome will do, but I recommend getting an electric one, not one of the old 'tick-tock' ones. The Korg MA-30 has some additional features that will be useful later. Most of my students have this metronome, and it is well-made and durable.

You can also find online metronomes if your budget is tight. My *Time Trainer Metronome* app is available for iOS and Android and has some extra features to help your timing.

Music Stand

A music stand can save your back. If you have any posture problems, get a stand now! Many people sit on the bed or the sofa with sheet music next to them and twist around to see it, craning their neck to look at their fingers. This puts you on a sure-fire track to expensive chiropractic bills. Get a stand—they are not expensive and will make your practice time more comfortable.

Justin Recommends: Any music stand!

Capo

A capo is a really cool device that you place on the guitar neck, and it changes the pitch of the open strings. They are used to change the key of a song, and will enable you to play along with songs that are otherwise very hard. If you sing, they are also useful to change the key of a song quickly to help you find the right key for your singing voice. A very useful (though not 100% necessary) accessory.

Justin Recommends: Kyser (I doubt you'll ever wear one out!)

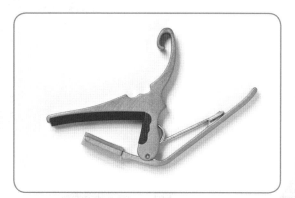

Display Folder (or ring binder)

It really helps you learn fast if you keep your notes organised. I recommend buying a clear display folder or a ring binder to keep all your notes in and keep them organised. It really will help; it somehow keeps your head tidy if your notes are tidy. They are not expensive, so give it a go.

Justin Recommends: Snowpake Display Folder

Recorder/Jam buddy/Looper

One of the best things you can do when you are learning is have a jam buddy that learns with you, a friend at about the same level that you can practise and learn with. It is also a massive advantage when it comes to learning to improvise because one person can play chords while the other learns to take a solo, and then swap. If you don't have this option I recommend getting a small recorder, so you can record yourself playing and then jam along with that. It is also a very good thing to hear yourself back, so a recorder is a great thing to have even if you have a jam buddy.

Another alternative is to buy a looper pedal, but for a beginner this would be a little over the top, and another thing to get your head around. I've been using the Boomerang III for a while now and love it, but they ain't cheap!

Justin Recommends: Find a friend :)

There is some more information on specific products from this range that I recommend on the web site at RE-020 • Recommended Products for Beginners.

Getting Started

Stage 1

Stage 2

Stage 3

Stage 4

Stage 5

Stage 6

Stage 7

Stage 8

Stage 9

Bonus

Getting Started

Stage 1
Stage 2
Stage 3
Stage 4
Stage 5
Stage 6
Stage 7
Stage 8
Stage 9
Bonus

Introduction

The anatomy of the guitar is pretty simple. Many guitar parts have names just like parts of the human body! These are some of the terms you will hear when people talk about guitars.

Fingerboard (or fretboard)
The part of the guitar where you place your fingers to play; the flatter side of the neck.

Body
The main part of the guitar, where you'll find the bridge, and on electric guitars, the volume and tone controls. This is easy to remember: the body is the bit that is in contact with your body!

Strap Pin
This is thing that your guitar strap fits on. I seriously recommend getting some kind of strap lock for this! (See page 16).

Input Jack Socket
This is where you will plug your guitar in if you use an amplifier. Make sure the cable is pushed all the way in or it will make a lot of noise!

Bridge
The far end of the strings from the nut, on the body of the guitar, usually metal. This is where the 'ball' will sit when you change your strings (see page 180).

Volume Knob(s)
Pretty obvious really: these control the volume of the electric signal of your guitar. If you've got more than one pickup, you'll usually have more than one volume knob (this is more often the case with Gibson-type guitars rather than Fenders)

Tone Knob(s)
Most guitars have one or two tone controls. These control the amount of bass (low) and treble (high) sounds that the guitar makes. Take some time to play a chord and move the tone knob so you know what it does, because you really have to hear it to understand!

Neck
The bit that pokes out of the body, which the strings run along.

1st fret

5th fret

12th fret

Headstock
The bit at the end of the neck where the strings stop and we find the tuners.

Position Markers
The dots on the fretboard are a handy indicator of the 3rd, 5th, 7th and 9th frets. The 12th fret has two dots; then the pattern repeats.

Fretwires
The small strips of metal that go across the fingerboard.

Frets
The spaces in between the fretwires*

Pickup(s)
A pickup is found under the strings of an electric guitar, and 'picks up' the sound. They contain magnets, and measure the changes of the magnetic field made by the moving strings. They come in two basic types: single coil (as found on most Fender guitars) and humbucker (found on most Gibson guitars). humbuckers have a fatter sound, and create less hum (hence the name).

Pickup Selector
Most electric guitars have more than one pickup, and the selector will allow you to choose which is being used. You can often choose to use more than one at a time. Fender Stratocasters have three pickups, but have a five-way switch. Gibson Les Pauls have two pickups and a three-way switch.

Scratch Plate
Scratch plates have a couple of functions. On acoustics they are there to protect the body and on electrics they hold all the electronics in place and protect the wood.

'Whammy' Bar
This is a metal bar that comes out of the bridge in some instruments and by pushing it down will lower the pitch of the notes being played. They can make your guitar go out of tune, and in my opinion are not a very useful attribute on a beginner's guitar, but they are a lot of fun and can be very expressive once you know what you are doing!

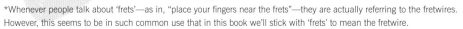

*Whenever people talk about 'frets'—as in, "place your fingers near the frets"—they are actually referring to the fretwires. However, this seems to be in such common use that in this book we'll stick with 'frets' to mean the fretwire.

Getting Started

Stage 1

Stage 2

Stage 3

Stage 4

Stage 5

Stage 6

Stage 7

Stage 8

Stage 9

Bonus

Tuners
The things that you turn to change the pitch of the strings. Usually found on the headstock.

Truss Rod Access
This allows you to correct any 'bow' in the neck. Best left to professional luthiers.

Nut
A bone or plastic (sometimes metal) piece at the end of the fingerboard near the headstock.

String Tree
Some guitars have a small 'tree' that the strings run under in between the nut and the tuning pegs, to keep the strings from jumping out of the nut. This isn't needed on most guitars.

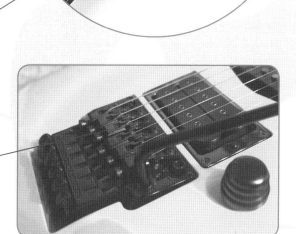

Floating tremolo
A type of bridge system whammy bar that locks the strings so that they don't go out of tune, a common problem when you use a whammy bar on a regular guitar. They are great if you are doing serious whammy bar tricks, like Steve Vai or Joe Satriani, but for the beginner they are usually a complete nightmare. None of my guitars have them because I don't play that style much, and my Jeff Beck Stratocaster is pretty good at staying in tune with a normal Fender bridge!

 ## Acoustic guitars

Most of the terms on these pages apply to both electric and acoustic guitars. Here are a few which are specific to acoustics:

Sound Hole
This is where the sound of the guitar will come out after it has bounced around inside! When you strum you don't want to cover this too much if you can help it.!

Rose
This is just decoration around the Sound Hole.

String Peg
A string peg is a plastic (or sometimes metal) pin that holds the string in the bridge. Make sure these are pressed in firmly because there is a lot of pressure on them and they can be dangerous if they spring out. Read the lesson on Changing Acoustic Strings (page 180) carefully before playing with these!

Making The Most Of Your Practice Time

Getting Started

Stage 1

Stage 2

Stage 3

Stage 4

Stage 5

Stage 6

Stage 7

Stage 8

Stage 9

Bonus

 ## Learning the guitar is going to take practice!

Here are some tips to help you make the most of your practice time. These are pretty important and will help you enjoy your time with your guitar—if you heed these tips, you will learn better and faster!

Justin's top ten practice tips

Included in this list are some things that may not be very useful for a beginner, but try to remember them for later. These are the Ten Commandments of practice!

1) Practise what you can't do, not what you can.

2) Never practise making a mistake. Get it right.

3) Start slowly and get it right before you speed up.

4) Using a timer saves time.

5) Focus on one element of practice at a time.

6) Try and practise a little every day, rather than practising a lot all on one day.

7) Keep track of your practice: use a practice schedule.

8) If it sounds good, it is good!

9) Playing and practising are very different—don't confuse them.

10) The more you think, the more you stink! Practise until it becomes instinctive.

A common question...

If I have more time than your suggested routines, what extra things should I practise?

The best thing to do would be to have a 10-minute break to let your head clear and then do the whole thing again!

An extra tip to keep your enjoyment levels at maximum:

Make sure you leave some time for fun in there too. Too much regimented practice and no fun could well make you lose interest. So, make sure you leave some time to jam around and play about—let your new skills grow your own way! Ideally, you would spend half the time you have to practise working on specific exercises and then that same amount of time again just playing around, noodling, experimenting and enjoying the new sounds you are making.

Remember that ticking boxes in a practice routine can be one of the best motivators you will find. You will be able to keep tabs on exactly how much work you are doing and make sure you are working on the right skills.

Sit up straight!

It is important to get into the habit of getting your body and finger positions right, which will help you play well. In this lesson we will talk about good posture and correct placement of your fretting fingers, which is **REALLY** important for beginners.

Sitting down to play

Classical posture Vs Rock posture

If you want to play classical guitar, then use the classical posture (put the guitar on the same leg as your fretting hand). If not then play the 'normal' way and place it on the same leg as your strumming hand. For right-handed players this means placing your guitar on your right leg.

This will give you a better posture for playing and I think it looks kind of strange when people play rock or pop with the classical posture. It just looks weird! That said, there are some amazing guitarists who play this way.

A bit awkward...

...that's better!

Raising the right leg (and crossing your legs)
I find it easier to keep an electric guitar cosy and tight if I lift my right leg a little (1). That usually means lifting my right knee a bit by putting my toes on the floor instead of the heel, sometimes with the heel resting on the chair leg. I'm not saying that you should, or have to do this, but sometimes I do, and there were a few questions about it on the forum.

1.

2.

The other alternative that achieves the same thing is to cross your right leg over your left (2). This kind of makes a little 'V' shape at your hip which helps hold the guitar securely; I like sitting like this, too!

Getting Started

Stage 1

Stage 2

Stage 3

Stage 4

Stage 5

Stage 6

Stage 7

Stage 8

Stage 9

Bonus

Getting Started

Stage 1
Stage 2
Stage 3
Stage 4
Stage 5
Stage 6
Stage 7
Stage 8
Stage 9
Bonus

 Playing standing up

Strap Placement and Standing Up

Set your strap so that the guitar is roughly in the same place when you stand as when you sit. This will make it a lot easier to play, unless you want to play with the strap low, and plan to always practise standing up (which is not recommended!).

Keeping the Neck Still

Make sure that your fretting hand is not supporting the guitar neck at all and that the neck is stable when you are playing. The last thing you want is the neck wobbling about when you are trying to practise getting your fingers in the right position.

Using A Mirror

If you have a bit of a belly, or find yourself straining your neck to see the fingerboard, you might consider using a mirror. I used my dad's shaving mirror when I first practised pretty much all of the time, so I could check the position of my fretting hand, but having a big mirror so you can see both hands and your posture is ideal.

Yes, I know it's not plugged in!

Many people develop tension in their shoulders when they play, especially when doing difficult things. Stay relaxed and you will make it easier for yourself. Imagine that your fretting hand is nailed to the neck and then just let the whole shoulder and elbow relax. It will help your fingers stretch as well: you will always get a better reach when you are relaxed.

Fretting Finger Position

Making sure that you understand why it is important to put your fingers just behind the fret is vital—if you know why, you are more likely to do it the right way. You need to play as close to the frets as you can (without actually touching the fret). This means that you don't have to press down too hard and your fingers will hurt less (although all beginners get sore fingers—this is normal—don't worry about it!). Pressing too hard will also make some notes go sharp, which will make your chords sound horrible, so really watch out for that.

Try pressing as lightly as you can near the fret while still getting a good, clear note. Then move your finger away from the fret, and notice how much more pressure you need to apply to get a good sound. As a beginner, you want to position your finger where you can get a good sound with the least pressure, which is next to the fret.

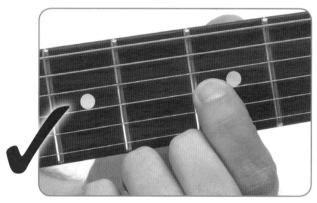

Do it this way!

Not this way!

Thumb Placement

Try and keep the thumb positioned behind the neck when you start. Later on you will probably bring it over to play particular chords, bass notes and all sorts of other tricks, but as a beginner, keep it behind the neck and it will help develop the muscles that you will need to play barre chords.

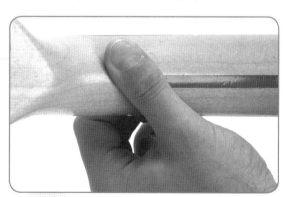

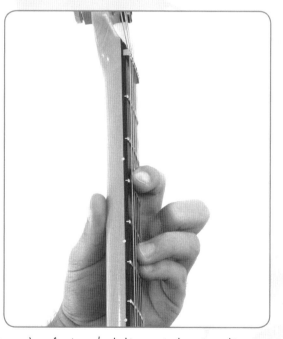

Your thumb position will vary depending upon what you're playing, but these photos show the basic position, which is the best starting point.

23

£10 music stand vs £1000 chiropractor bill...

Having your sheet music or book sitting next to you on the bed or sofa and twisting around to see it is a sure-fire way to give yourself neck and back problems later in life, and I can assure you that the small investment of a music stand is well worth it. You don't need a fancy one; just the basic fold-up type is fine.

Keep the nails short on your fretting hand

I already mentioned this, but you should make sure that you keep your nails nice and short, or the nail will dig into the wood of the fingerboard and make your fingers lie too flat. You should use the tips of your fingers to play the notes when you start. Later you might start to use them a little flatter, but learn to use the tips first.

You'd smile too if you could see what I was reading from!

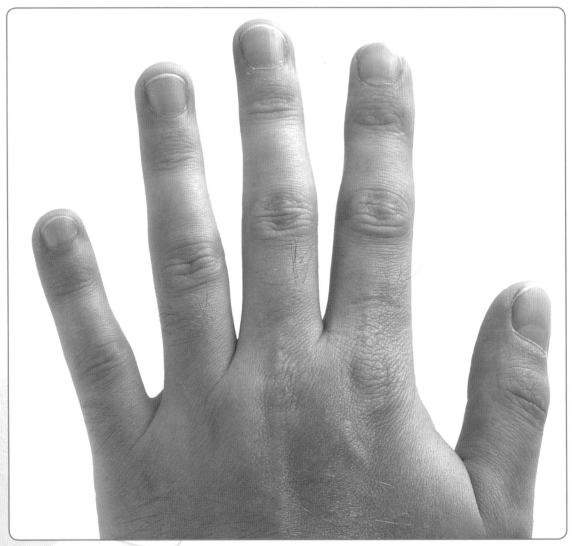

Nice, short fingernails.

Questions from the forum that I think will help you, too!

I started playing classical-style with the guitar on my left leg. I think I should switch, but it's hard. Help!

If you started playing with a 'classical' posture then your hands will be used to playing that way and making the switch will feel difficult, but not for long. As with most things, when you try something new it usually takes a little getting used to, and this is no exception. You should find that after a few weeks of playing it will feel better and you'll probably have a hard time going back to the old way. That said, some people simply prefer playing with the classical posture, and that is fine too.

How does one go about holding top-heavy guitars?

Top heavy guitars (where the headstock is heavy and the neck pulls toward the ground) can be a pain. My Gibson Les Paul Gold Top is really top heavy and the only thing I have found to help is to use a strap and stand up. I don't practise a lot with Les Pauls for this reason, but I know other people who love the feel of them, so it's just a preference I guess.

When I place all four fingers on the fretboard, my index finger tilts inward towards/away from my other fingers. Is this bad?

Everybody's hands are a little different, don't worry about it! There are some guitar freaks out there that seem to have 'guitar-shaped' hands with perfectly even finger lengths, that seem to be able to stretch to grab any chord with ease, but that's not the case for most players. I have a tiny little finger, but I don't find many chord grips I can't play... I've seen dudes with HUGE 'farmer's fingers' that can still play intricate jazz grips and little kids playing amazingly difficult stretches with tiny hands... it just takes practice!

How exactly should the tip of the finger be positioned on the string? How near or far from the nail must the string be?

This picture will show you:

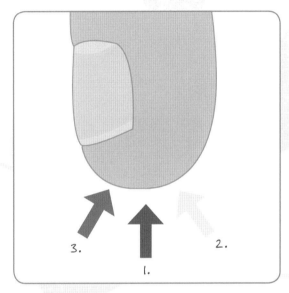

The problem is that this changes depending on what you are playing. As a beginner, you probably should be aiming to press the string at arrow 1; as you progress, you'll move a little bit more towards arrow 2 (or past it) because you'll use the tip of the finger to mute other strings. DO NOT try this if you are a beginner, it'll screw up your technique! If your finger is pressing the string at 3. it will hurt, and is not recommended!

My hand touches the neck just next to the high E string. Is this a really bad habit?

As a beginner, yes, you should avoid this. You will probably find that your hand will often mute the thin E string, and also hinder your chord change speed. Later on, you might find that it's O.K. to have the hand gripping there, but you are better off not learning that way. This is one of those things that will change as you develop your guitar playing, but you can't start like that, and you may also find that your hand is supporting the neck, which is bad as well.

Getting Started

Stage 1

Stage 2

Stage 3

Stage 4

Stage 5

Stage 6

Stage 7

Stage 8

Stage 9

Bonus

Getting
Started

Stage 1
Stage 2
Stage 3
Stage 4
Stage 5
Stage 6
Stage 7
Stage 8
Stage 9
Bonus

Pick one up and bash the strings with it!

O.K. Nearly there! I always recommend that you use a pick when you first start learning to play, and learn fingerstyle later (but it is up to you of course...) and so we just need to make sure that that you are holding the pick correctly.

Holding The Pick

Hold the pick so that it comes out of the side of your thumb and hold it with the tip of the 1st finger (see the pictures below). The rest of your hand should just be relaxed. Make sure that the pick is coming out of the side of your thumb—this is by far the most important aspect of the correct position.

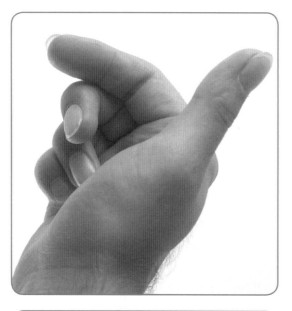
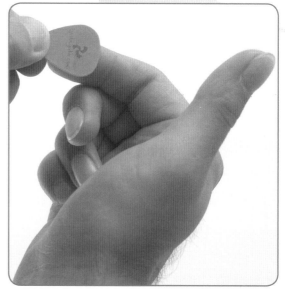
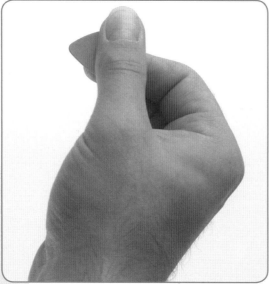

This is what it should look like if you are holding the pick correctly to play.

Recommended picks

Jim Dunlop Nylon

Gauge: .38mm or .46mm

These are very thin and great for strumming. However, any very thin pick will be fine; just try and get as thin as possible. I think this type should be first choice for a beginner guitar player, as they are very forgiving when you are learning to strum. You might find it easier to use a medium gauge (below) when you start to play individual notes.

Jim Dunlop Tortex

Gauge: .60mm

These are a little thicker; they're better for playing one note at a time but require more control and therefore are not so good for absolute beginners learning to strum.

Jim Dunlop Jazz III

Gauge: 1.38mm

This is a very thick pick that I use for electric playing. I never use it for playing acoustic guitar, as it sounds kind of dead, or flat, and has no percussive 'click', but they are great for electric guitar. The thicker pick gives excellent control for complex stuff too.

I use them for both rhythm and lead playing on electric, and as it happens, the vast majority of pro players I know use this same pick!

Really spend the time to learn how to hold the pick properly when you first start out.

Getting Started

Stage 1

Stage 2

Stage 3

Stage 4

Stage 5

Stage 6

Stage 7

Stage 8

Stage 9

Bonus

Picks: How To Choose One And Hold It (Cont'd)

Getting Started

Stage 1

Stage 2

Stage 3

Stage 4

Stage 5

Stage 6

Stage 7

Stage 8

Stage 9

Bonus

 F.A.Qs. answered

My pick seems to turn around in my hand, what is going on?

This is really common when you start out. If you try and hold the pick too hard then your arm will feel tense; if you hold it too loose, then it falls out or turns around. The solution is practice. Don't let it worry you in the early stages; it will simply take a while for your hand to deal with holding the pick with exactly the right amount of pressure.

What angle should the pick hit the strings?

When you are strumming with a light pick, the angle of picking is not too important. However, if you feel like your pick is getting stuck in the strings, it might be because you are angling the pick in such a way that it's getting caught up.

To get it right: start by lining up the pick with the strings, and then turn it so that the pick is angled down just a bit, say 15 degrees. This way the pick will glide over the strings rather than getting caught up in them. If the pick is strumming flat (parallel) against the strings it often gets hooked into the strings and makes your rhythm playing kinda lumpy. So you need to keep the pick at an angle so it will move easily over the strings.

I sometimes find my 2nd finger holding the pick too: is that bad?

Yes it is. Try and hold the pick with just your thumb and 1st finger. Using other fingers will most likely put your wrist at a strange angle and cause problems when you try to develop your technique further. That said, many great players use strange techniques and hold the pick funny, but what

This is the right angle for the pick to hit the strings.

justinguitar.com

Getting Started

Stage 1

Stage 2

Stage 3

Stage 4

Stage 5

Stage 6

Stage 7

Stage 8

Stage 9

Bonus

I always recommend is starting the 'right' way and really giving it a good go before you decide it doesn't work for you. George Benson holds his pick kind of upside down; Brian May uses a coin and Jeff Beck gave up on using the pick altogether, so it really is your decision in the end. Often, people who start out using a thicker pick try and use three fingers to hold onto it when they strum. A better solution is just to use a thinner pick and hold it the right way!

Using your 2nd finger to hold the pick will:
- Change the angle of your hand, and so change the angle that the pick hits the strings, in a bad way.
- Change the angle of your palm, which makes it hard to do palm muting.
- Make 'hybrid' picking almost impossible, if you decide to get into that later.
- Mean that you can't use your 2nd finger for tapping.
- Hinder your ability to manipulate the pick.

I know the 'right' way can feel really weird if you started using three fingers to hold the pick, but I really think it's worth trying to get back to holding it with just your thumb and 1st finger. It will take a bit of time to get used to how hard to hold it. Like everything else, it's gonna take some practice!

Do I need to hold it differently when I strum?

Yes. When you pick out notes one at a time, you don't want too much pick poking out, but when you strum it's ok to have a lot more pick showing from out of your thumb. As you play more you will learn to manipulate how much of the pick sticks out while you play; this sounds hard but it will just happen naturally. Don't stress about it! It will happen when it's ready, and not a second earlier…

I like the 'back in the old days' style, is it really bad to hold the pick at the knuckle?

Well, no—there are many great players that played that way—but there are issues with it. I recently taught a guy who showed up with blood all over his guitar because his knuckle was hitting the strings a lot. That's no good. It also makes it hard to use 'circle' picking which is a more advanced technique you certainly won't be doing in the beginner's course, but is very useful later on when you want to start speeding things up a bit!

I like the Jazz III but they feel too small for strumming…

Then try the Jazz III XL, which is the same shape and thickness, but a bit bigger; lots of people like them.

When I do a lot of strumming (with a pick) the nail on my index finger gets worn down quite a lot, it's kind of towards the right side (or bottom as I'm playing). Is this normal? Am I doing something wrong?

That means you are letting your finger hit the strings when you strum. This is a very bad habit; you need to adjust your finger position on the pick and the angle of your hand as you are doing your down-strums. You would be better off trying to fix this now rather than later. Go back to doing it nice and slowly and make sure that is not happening. It's going to be a bit tough to make the change but it's definitely worth it. If you don't stop it now it will affect your sound later, and you'll hurt your fingers if you practise a lot.

Getting Started

Stage 1
Stage 2
Stage 3
Stage 4
Stage 5
Stage 6
Stage 7
Stage 8
Stage 9
Bonus

 Gotta learn how to read them...

You are going to be reading chord boxes in the very first stage so you will need to get this down now. You won't need to read tab for a little while yet, but we'll give you a brief run down of it here so you at least understand the basics of this as well. I do not encourage beginners to read music notation, because it makes for very slow progress.

 Reading chord boxes

The first thing that you need to know is how to read chord boxes. These show you where to put your fingers on the fingerboard to play chords. The six vertical lines represent the six strings. The string on the furthest left is the thickest string (E). The thick line at the top of the box represents the nut (the plastic, bone or metal piece that the strings go through on the headstock) and the rest of the horizontal lines represent the frets.

The dots represent the places where you put your left-hand fingers, and they are numbered to show which finger to use. Number 1 is the index finger, 2 is the middle finger, 3 is the ring finger and 4 is your pinky (little finger). If you have played the piano make sure you don't get confused; piano finger numbering is completely different (guitar players generally don't use their left-hand thumbs).

Notice the X or O above each string too. These show whether you should play the string or not for that chord. The O means that you play the string 'open'—with no fingers holding it down—and the X means that you should not play that string.

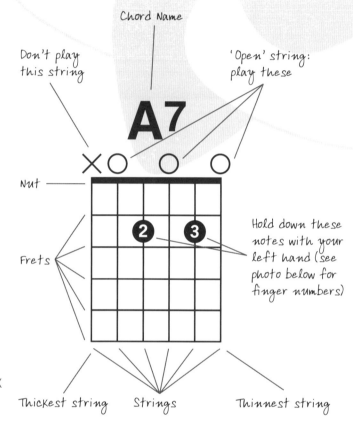

Chord Name

Don't play this string

'Open' string: play these

A7

Nut

Frets

Hold down these notes with your left hand (see photo below for finger numbers)

Thickest string   Strings   Thinnest string

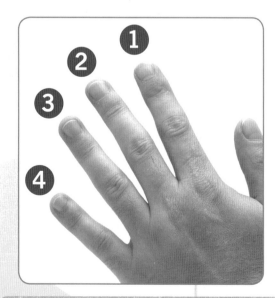

Make sure you carefully check which strings you're meant to play for each chord.

justinguitar.com

Getting Started

Stage 1

Stage 2

Stage 3

Stage 4

Stage 5

Stage 6

Stage 7

Stage 8

Stage 9

Bonus

This is how you'll see the chord shapes displayed in this book. Each chord diagram is accompanied by at least one photo of the correct finger position. There's actually a bit of a problem with using photos to show you how to play chords, because the fingers that you're not using might be hiding your view of where your other fingers are placed. Where this is the case, we've used more than one picture; one that makes the finger position completely clear, by deliberately pulling your unused finger(s) out of the way and one that shows you what the chord will look like when you're actually playing.

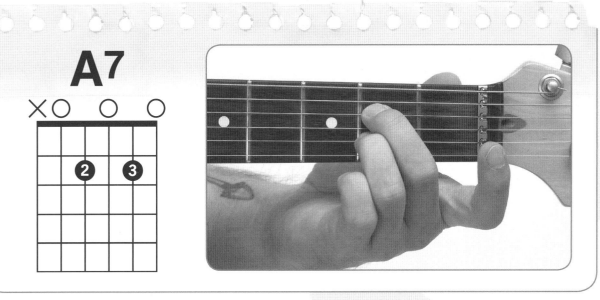

You'll notice that the photos show you the chord as if you were looking at someone else playing, rather than yourself. This is because you shouldn't actually be able to see the whole of your left hand if you are holding the guitar properly (see page 23). You'd have to angle the neck, which creates the wrong posture for your wrist. If you're having trouble with getting your fingers in the right place, try using a mirror to make sure your chord shapes are correct. For the early stages I also show you how the chord should look like to you when you're playing—from above—and also the best place to put your thumb behind the neck.

Reading TAB

Guitar TAB (or guitar tablature) is a way of writing music specifically for guitar. It is perfect for those that do not read music, and in many cases offers more information than the written notation would anyway!

TAB has six horizontal lines that represent the six strings on the guitar.
The top line is the thinnest string (first) and the lowest line represents the thickest (sixth) string.
The numbers that are placed on the lines tell you what fret to play a note. You will only ever play the strings with numbers on; If a string has no number, don't play it.
The 0 means that a string is played open, with no fingers pressing down the string on the frets.

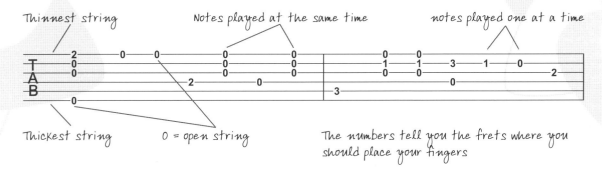

Getting Your Guitar In Tune

Getting Started

Stage 1

Stage 2

Stage 3

Stage 4

Stage 5

Stage 6

Stage 7

Stage 8

Stage 9

Bonus

Your guitar will sound a lot better if it is in tune!

Tuning is an important skill to learn, but takes practice just like everything else, so I do advise beginners to get a guitar tuner so they can make the guitar sound as nice as possible, for you and anyone that has to listen to you practise!

Using a tuner

It's my opinion that beginner guitarists should use an electric tuner. Learning to tune takes some time and I think it's better if a student has some time to hear a guitar in tune before starting work learning to tune themselves. It's also a lot better for those that have to listen as well!

Tuners are not expensive these days and there are some brilliant ones available as iPhone apps now. Check out the Peterson iStroboSoft tuner—it's as good and fast as the pro Peterson tuners I use— in fact I use it more and more these days as it's always in my pocket!

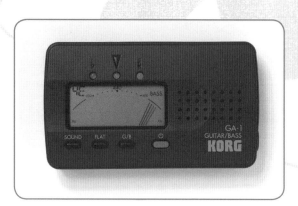

Tuning to reference notes

CD 1 Track 1

Using reference notes to tune is a very useful skill, and one you can learn during this course using the tuning notes found on CD 1 on Track 1. To use this method, listen to the reference note and then tune the corresponding string up or down to match. It will take some practice to be able to do this quickly and accurately, but it's a skill you will often use if you want to play with another musician (especially if they can't change their tuning easily, like piano players!).

Tuning to a piano

Tuning to piano is the same as above really, but instead of using a reference track on a CD of another guitar, you play notes on a piano. You will learn the notes of the open strings on the guitar soon (so you can ask a piano player to "give me an A") or you can use the chart to play them yourself. The thinnest string is the pitch E above 'Middle' C. (Hint: hold down the sustain pedal under the piano so the note rings out after you have taken your finger off the key to tune your guitar!).

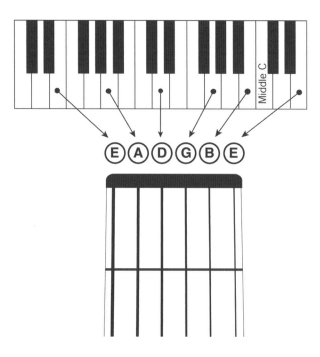

Tuning to pitch pipes

Pitch pipes were what I had with my first guitar! They are like a harmonica but they only have six notes, which match up with the six strings of the guitar. They are popular because they are small, cheap and you can hold it in your mouth and blow while you use your hands to tune up… but I still think getting a tuner is a better option.

Relative tuning

If you don't have access to a tuner, or any other reference to tune to, you can use this method to get your instrument in tune with itself. Because most notes on the guitar can be found in more than one place on the neck, it is possible to use 'relative' tuning. To do this you need the thickest E string to be at least roughly in tune. Then, by playing the note at the 5th fret of the sixth (the thickest) string, you can tune the open fifth string up or down until it sounds the same: they are both the note A. Once that is good, play the 5th fret of the fifth string, and tune the open fourth string so that it sounds the same, and so on as per the diagram. Note that to tune the second string you place your finger in the 4th fret of the third string, not at the 5th, which is the case for all the other strings.

Tuning with harmonics

There is one more advanced tuning method commonly used and that is using harmonics. This is something you will learn later. There is a lesson on this on the website and I suggest you have a look at it after you have finished the beginner's course.

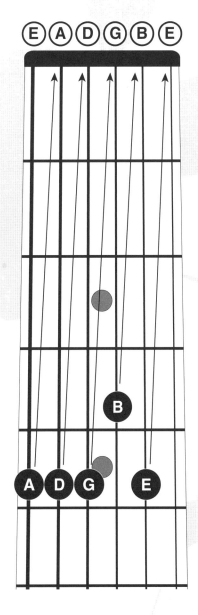

That's it! Let's learn how to play!

Getting Started

Stage 1
Stage 2
Stage 3
Stage 4
Stage 5
Stage 6
Stage 7
Stage 8
Stage 9
Bonus

Stage 1

Getting Started

Stage 1

Stage 2

Stage 3

Stage 4

Stage 5

Stage 6

Stage 7

Stage 8

Stage 9

Bonus

 ## Right—deep breath, and let's get started...

We're about to start playing, so relax and enjoy. Take it easy! Don't push your fingers until they hurt; if they get sore, then go and make a cup of tea and come back to it later.

It's a wonderful journey but you have to start slow. Doing too many hours of practice in the very early stages usually just leads to pain and frustration, so I would recommend no more than 30 minutes a day at the absolute maximum for the first couple of weeks, at least.

It is totally normal to feel completely useless the first few times you try and play. Some people pick it up right away, but most don't. So allow yourself some time and don't waste energy worrying about anything. Let the guitar be your stress reliever, the thing you do to relax, not your taskmaster!

Remember that you are asking your fingers to do strange things they have most likely not done before. Using soft flesh to press down metal wires is not going to feel great until the skin toughens up.

You are also likely to think to yourself "It's impossible to stretch my fingers out to make this chord". But you will find it easy in a few weeks. Just keep trying the best you can and your fingers will soon limber up!

BC-117

Here is a list of 10 songs—all included in the Justinguitar.com Beginner's Songbook—which you can play using the chords we'll cover in this stage:

Three Little Birds (Bob Marley & The Wailers)

Feelin' Alright (Traffic)

Hound Dog (Elvis Presley)

Walk Of Life (Dire Straits)

I Walk The Line (Johnny Cash)

The Gambler (Kenny Rogers)

Blowin' In The Wind (Bob Dylan)

Love Me Do (The Beatles)

How Bizarre (OMC)

Common People (Pulp)

Getting Started

Stage 1

Stage 2

Stage 3

Stage 4

Stage 5

Stage 6

Stage 7

Stage 8

Stage 9

Bonus

The D Chord

Getting Started

Stage 1

Stage 2

Stage 3

Stage 4

Stage 5

Stage 6

Stage 7

Stage 8

Stage 9

Bonus

OK, time to get your fingers on the guitar and make a sound! So grab your guitar and let's go...

Look at the chord box for the D chord below. The black dots are the places where you should position your fretting fingers.

CD 1 Track **2**

D

Place your fingers as shown in the chord box and photo above. Most students find it is easier to arrange their fingers by number order, starting with your 1st finger. This method isn't that important, but try it and see if it works for you. Place your 1st finger on the third string, 2nd fret, the 2nd finger on the first string—also on the 2nd fret—and your 3rd finger on the second string on the 3rd fret.

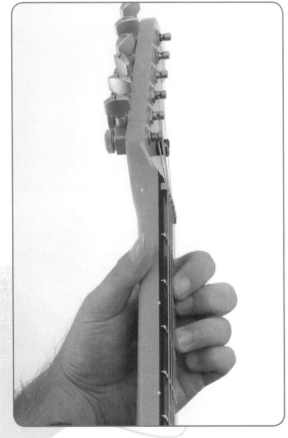

Your fingers should be placed just behind the fret. If a finger is touching the fret, the note will sound dead or muted and if it is too far back from the wire the note will buzz.
You may find that your fingers will not stretch to where you want them to go at first, but it won't take long for them to find the way to play it. Just let your hand get used to moving in ways that it may never have done before!

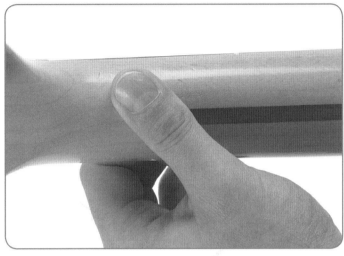

Thumb position

When you start playing it is better to keep your thumb placed behind the neck. Have it resting about 3/4 of the way towards the sixth (thickest) string, firmly planted on the pad of the thumb (not the tip). Your palm should not be touching anywhere. Got that? THE PALM OF YOUR LEFT HAND MUST NOT BE TOUCHING THE NECK! THIS IS REALLY IMPORTANT!

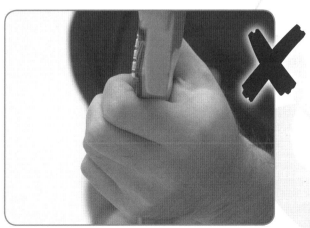

Like this: you can see space between the neck and your palm.

Not like this: gripping the neck right up against your palm.

Getting Started

Stage 1

Stage 2

Stage 3

Stage 4

Stage 5

Stage 6

Stage 7

Stage 8

Stage 9

Bonus

The D Chord (Cont'd.)

Getting
Started

Stage 1

Stage 2

Stage 3

Stage 4

Stage 5

Stage 6

Stage 7

Stage 8

Stage 9

Bonus

What strings do I play?

Check which strings should be played, and which strings you're going to leave. For the D chord, you should NOT play the thickest two strings. Remember, the X above a string in the chord box means that you don't play that string.

Have a go now and strum down with your pick from the fourth string down (towards the ground), remembering that the sixth string is the thickest string.

When you strum, be aware of where you start the strum from. Although it may seem like a lot to think about just now, the eventual quality of your playing will be worth the little extra time to get it right. It will be tempting sometimes to just disregard it and strum away on your favourite tune. When this urge hits you, just do it. But when you PRACTISE then you need to very be careful about which notes you are hitting. Have a listen to what our D chord sounds like if all six strings are plucked: pretty rough, and it makes the chord muddy and unclear.

Get the notes clear

What you may need to do now is make some adjustments. Don't worry if the ends of your fingers get a bit sore. Take a short break if it bothers you too much. Check that each finger is not touching anywhere it should not. On this D chord it is quite common for your 3rd finger to be touching the first string, and stopping it sounding. If this is the case then try to angle the finger more directly down on the string with the tip of your finger. Try to let there be a small gap between the edge of your 1st finger and the fingerboard. Again, the palm of your hand should not be touching the guitar neck at all.

Strum/pick out/strum

One of the most important beginner's skills is to get your chords clear. I always teach students to "strum, pick out, strum". This is the best way to check your chords and get them correct. You will use this method for all chords that you learn in the future! This is how all the chords are demonstrated on the CD.

Start by giving the chord a strum, then play each note individually, starting from the thickest string that you should play. Make any necessary adjustments that you need to get every note ringing clearly and then strum the chord again. Take a break, and then try it again.

The hard part is getting the notes clear when you pick them one at a time. What might have sounded like a good chord on that first strum can have quite a few notes missing that you will only discover when you try and pick them one at a time.

As you strum it the second time after the corrections, with all the notes nice and clear, tell yourself that this is how you want the chord to sound. This will take some practice. There is no shortcut—you just have to put in the time to get it right.

Getting Started · Stage 1 · Stage 2 · Stage 3 · Stage 4 · Stage 5 · Stage 6 · Stage 7 · Stage 8 · Stage 9 · Bonus

Alternative fingerings

You will find that there are other ways that you could finger each chord shape, and you might even find it easier another way. However, I strongly suggest that you start with the fingering that I show you here. It is going to help you with your chord changes and almost everyone plays the D chord this way. James Taylor is the only big-name player I can think of that plays it differently. He swaps the 1st and 2nd fingers over, which is very unusual, and not recommended for beginners.

It hurts!

Your first chord is going to hurt. Sorry! Pressing your soft skin down on thin metal strings is going to be uncomfortable when you start. Everyone has to go through it, but it doesn't last! Remember not to play too much and wear out the skin or you'll have to have a few weeks off to let them heal. Just play a bit until they get sore, have a little rest and then come back to it.

It usually takes a month for the fingers to get used to it, though you should find it a lot less painful after just a couple of weeks.

Memory

You must try and memorise every chord you learn right away! You shouldn't need to look at this page after a week (at the very most) of playing. Try and get it into your head in 5 minutes or less. Just do it. It's no good having to look at the page—you will probably want to look at your fingers while you play when you start, and you can't look at both!

Strum this chord and play around with getting it sounding nice for 5 minutes or so. Have a bit of a play around and see what it sounds like.

Once you have this pretty much under your fingers (don't worry about getting it absolutely perfect just yet!) then it's time to check out another chord: A

The A Chord

Getting Started

Stage 1

Stage 2

Stage 3

Stage 4

Stage 5

Stage 6

Stage 7

Stage 8

Stage 9

Bonus

The next chord...

Unfortunately, I'm not aware of any one-chord songs, so now we have to move onto our next two chords so you can start playing some tunes. The next chord we are going to check out is the A chord.

CD 1 Track
3

A

With this chord, all your fingers are at the 2nd fret. Your 1st finger is placed on the third string; your 2nd finger on the fourth string; your 3rd finger on the second string. The first (thinnest) and fifth strings are played open. Don't play the thickest (sixth) string.

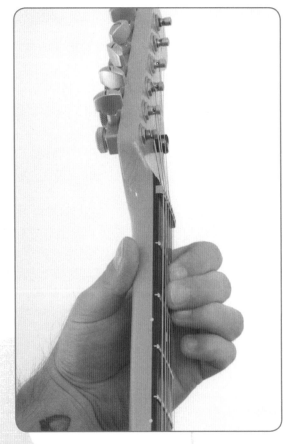

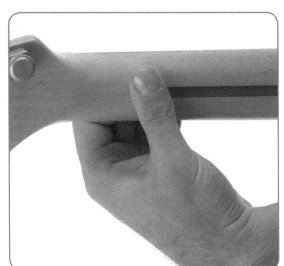

You should not pick the sixth string; all the rest should sound. Put your fingers down and then strum, check each individual note, and then strum again. Later you might use your thumb to mute the sixth string, but keep your thumb behind the neck for now to build up that muscle in between your thumb and your 1st finger. It should start getting a bit tired if you are doing it right!

Watch that your 3rd finger is not touching the first string, and that your fingers are pressing hard enough to get all the notes sounding out. This chord can take bit of adjustment to get right. Check that your left-hand palm is not touching the neck; your thumb should be supporting your hand.

It's normal at this stage for your fingers to be hurting really bad, for notes not to be coming out clearly, and a feeling that you might never get it. Pretty much everyone got that feeling when they started, I sure did! Just stick with it. It just takes practice. When your fingers are not yet toughened up, the soft pads spread out and touch the strings in places they shouldn't. Sometimes you won't be able to press hard enough to get a good note.

Don't worry about it—it will come—it's just going to need more hours of pain to get through to enjoying it!

The traditional approach (which I taught for many years) has the 1st, 2nd and 3rd fingers in a row at the 2nd fret (see below). However, now I prefer this newer fingering, where you swap around your 1st and 2nd fingers. This makes all the fingers closer to the frets, getting fingers two and three right next to the fretwire, with the 1st finger just pushing in from behind.

I would recommend that you use the new method. If you have learned the traditional way them stick with that —it's O.K.—I learnt using the traditional fingering. Later I will show you an easier and more useful way to play it.

I would strongly recommend that you don't get into using a mini-barre at this stage (just in case you have seen it somewhere else). It is a cool technique to use later, but for learning chord changes, getting your finger positions correct, and above all, to toughen them up, you are best off starting with the A fingering shown here.

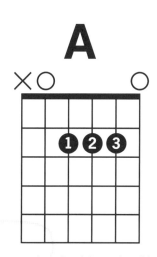

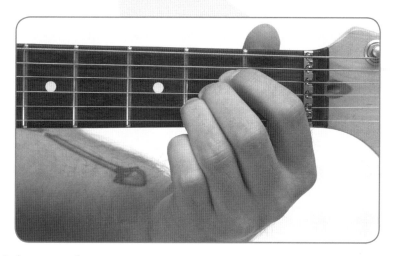

This is the traditional, 'old skool' fingering for A which you might have seen elsewhere. By the way, the tattoo on my arm is a broken arrow - not a 'long mushroom' as some of you have suggested!

When you have this one sorted it is time to get onto the next chord: E

Getting Started
Stage 1
Stage 2
Stage 3
Stage 4
Stage 5
Stage 6
Stage 7
Stage 8
Stage 9
Bonus

Getting Started

Stage 1

Stage 2

Stage 3

Stage 4

Stage 5

Stage 6

Stage 7

Stage 8

Stage 9

Bonus

Just one more chord for this stage and then we are going to be able to play some songs...

...after we have done a bit of work on changing between the chords!

CD 1 Track 4

E

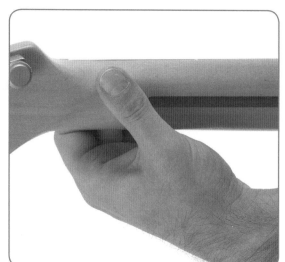

Arrange your fingers as shown on the neck diagram and then strum, check each note individually and then strum again. Check that your 1st finger is not touching on any of the strings that are played open and check that all the strings are sounding clear. This chord is made easier by the fact that all the strings are played.

It is very important that you commit all your chords to **MEMORY.**

It's often around about this time that people get the feeling that their hands are too small or too big, or that their fingers are too short, too long, too weak, too strong etc. It's nothing to worry about. Over the years I've taught young kids with tiny hands that managed amazing stretches, and players with fingers thicker than my arms, and they have all got there in the end! We all have different battles that we have to overcome. Some of us are too busy, some of have poor quality instruments, some have a short attention span, other lose heart easily. One thing is for sure: none of us are perfect, and part of the fun of learning music (in my humble opinion) is overcoming these setbacks and getting on with it and eventually becoming better people, stronger for the battles we have won.

Neil Finn says that "Everything is good for you, if it doesn't kill you"; when it comes to guitar, I think "Everything is good for you, as long as it doesn't make you give up!".

So hang in there—it really does get a lot easier after the first month or two!

When you have this chord under your fingers it's time to check out some cool tricks to help you change between A, D and E.

Getting Started

Stage 1

Stage 2

Stage 3

Stage 4

Stage 5

Stage 6

Stage 7

Stage 8

Stage 9

Bonus

Getting Started

Stage 1

Stage 2

Stage 3

Stage 4

Stage 5

Stage 6

Stage 7

Stage 8

Stage 9

Bonus

Use the anchor to guide the change!

Using your 1st finger as an 'anchor' will help you move between your chords smoothly.

Keeping your 1st finger on the third string (G) will help you guide all of your fingers to the next position when you change chords. You don't need to keep the pressure down, but leave it in contact with the string all the time.

Start with a change from A to E. After a few times changing between them I'm sure you will find that the anchor finger makes it a lot easier to make the change.

Try and maintain your accuracy as best you can while doing this stuff. The next thing we're going to look at is developing speed, (getting your chord changes faster) where accuracy is less important, but for other things, try and keep it as correct as you can!

Put your fingers down for the A (1.); then lift your 2nd and 3rd fingers, while leaving the 1st finger in its place. Slide the 1st finger back one fret to the 1st fret (2.), and then place your 2nd and 3rd fingers down in the correct frets to form an E chord (3.).

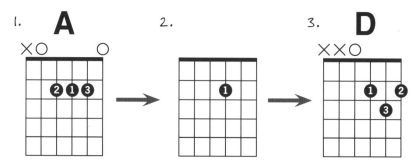

Once you are cool with that, have a go at using the same technique to change from A to D. This time the 1st finger will stay in the same place. Try it.

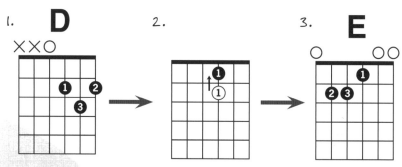

Once you are there with that, then move onto changing between D and E, still using your 1st finger as an anchor.

At this point I still recommend trying to get your fingers down one at a time, usually in finger order, starting with your 1st finger, then 2nd and then 3rd finger, just for consistency. It wouldn't make much difference really if you want to put them

down the other way round but you have the 1st finger down first for the anchor idea to work. This concept can be used any time a finger needs to stay on a string. It only works with certain chord changes, but use it where you can.

Remember too that at the start you are bound to make little mistakes. Be patient with yourself and enjoy the journey. Little mistakes will get corrected with time and practice, so don't beat yourself up if you have not mastered the guitar in the first week. It may take a little longer!

One-Minute Changes

Changing chords as fast as you can!

Once you know how to play your chords, the big challenge is to get the change from one chord to another fast enough so you can play a song without stopping between chords. You should be able to do this well before you start trying to play strumming patterns, or your songs will always sound disjointed and kind of silly!

The big trick is to really focus on a particular chord change for one minute, using either a stopwatch or a countdown timer. I use the countdown timer on my phone, but any one will do.

The concept is simple: time yourself for one minute and see how many changes between two chords you can do in that time. This works better than any other method I have ever heard of. It's really quite astounding how well this trick works. I started teaching it as a game for kids, but have since applied it to anyone learning guitar and is one of the key lessons in the whole beginner's course, so check it out, use it regularly and it will really help you develop your chord-changing skills.

There are three One-Minute Changes to practise at this stage:

D to A Your 1st finger will stay in the 2nd fret but you might have to move it a little within the fret.

D to E Make sure the 1st finger is in the right place before you put the rest of the fingers down.

A to E Don't put your first finger too close to the 2nd fret when moving to the A chord; for this chord finger 1 can't be right next to the fret.

Use the practice schedule (page 51) and write down how many times you make the change each session. You will find that being able to watch your progress will really help keep you motivated. Count '1' for each change; so D–A–D–A = four changes.

You will find this will make a HUGE difference if you stick to doing it every day, I see great results with this all the time with private students and I know you will see a fast improvement too!

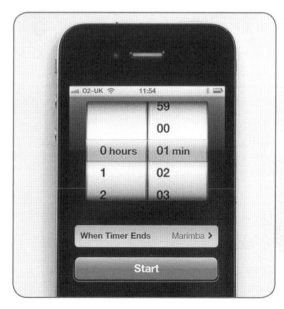

Use a timer, and play as many chord changes in one minute as you can.

Getting Started

Stage 1

Stage 2

Stage 3

Stage 4

Stage 5

Stage 6

Stage 7

Stage 8

Stage 9

Bonus

Four-To-The-Bar Strumming

Getting Started

Stage 1

Stage 2

Stage 3

Stage 4

Stage 5

Stage 6

Stage 7

Stage 8

Stage 9

Bonus

 ## Gotta be easy to strum down four times in a row, right?

For many people, strumming rhythms are the trickiest thing to learn so we are going to start very simply to build a solid foundation. This is very easy and I hope that none of you have too much of a problem with this one. The hard part is in keeping the timing as consistent as possible.

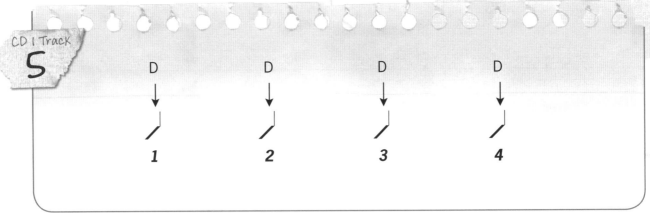

CD 1 Track

5

| D | D | D | D |
| 1 | 2 | 3 | 4 |

 A bar is a great place to have a drink. It is also a musical term that we use to divide time in music.

We have to check out the beats in the bar so we know how many times to strum our chords.

For now, all bars will contain four beats because playing four beats in a bar is by far the most common beat in music. There are other time signatures (bars that have a different number of beats in them) but we'll be saving them for a lot later. The count is "1, 2, 3, 4". For now, that is all we are looking at. All I want you to do is to be able to strum down four times, while you count along. Easy! Have a listen to the CD and try and copy what you hear, strumming an E chord.

It really helps to count along as you play so you always know where the bar starts. When we start playing songs, you will find that we nearly always change chord at the start of a bar, so it is very important that you know where '1' is.

We'll be looking at some harder rhythms later, but what you should be doing here is trying to get this very simple idea deep in your mind so that you just do it naturally and don't have to think about it. Use all down-strums and keep the strumming consistent. Try and keep the strumming at an even volume too.

Many people find it hard to hold on to the pick. If you hold it too tight, your playing will be tense and jerky; too loose, and you'll keep dropping it! The secret? Don't worry about it! It will come with time and practice.

justinguitar.com

Getting Started

Stage 1

Stage 2

Stage 3

Stage 4

Stage 5

Stage 6

Stage 7

Stage 8

Stage 9

Bonus

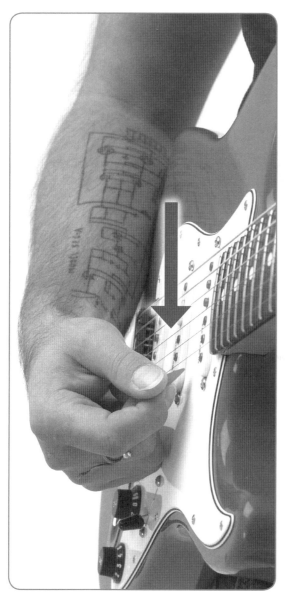

Strum down...

...and lift your hand up in between. Easy!

Getting Started

Stage 1

Stage 2

Stage 3

Stage 4

Stage 5

Stage 6

Stage 7

Stage 8

Stage 9

Bonus

Just Use Sound To Improve Now!

CD 1 Track 6

Music is about sound and listening, so this part of your guitar study will help you a lot more than you will initially realise. Many people never grasp the essential technique of learning songs by ear, but I believe that it is one of the most important skills that you can develop as a musician. But it is hard! People like me, that learnt before the internet, had to be either shown a song by a friend or work it out by ear. Every single guitarist that I have ever met that I have thought to be any good had transcribed lots of songs. Transcribing is working out a song using your ear and then writing it down. This could mean working out every single note of a guitar solo, but also refers to working out the chords and rhythm patterns to play for a song. This is a great skill to start developing as a beginner, rather than waiting until later in your guitar playing career.

It is hard to just jump in the deep end and work songs out without knowing what the possible chords are or how they might be played. So we'll start in this course by playing some chords from a set palette for you to identify. This will help you

realise that you can learn to do it, and I hope that by the end of the course you will be able to work out basic songs on your own.

It does take practice, in fact more than we can cover here, so you will need to do some work on your own. You could try and replicate the lessons that I present here by recording yourself, waiting a few days and then trying to work out the answers, or you could get a friend to play chords and chord sequences for you to work out. I prefer this 'jam buddy' method because it is always more fun working with another musician.

Make sure you do ALL the exercises in each test before checking the answers!

We'll start with two exercises: Single Sound Recognition and Chord Progression Recognition.

Single Sound Recognition (SSR)

On the CD you'll hear me play a chord—and then you have to work out what chord it is. To start with, do this by trying to find the chord on your guitar. Eventually—and this may take quite some time—you'll be able to tackle exercises like this without touching your guitar at all, as you learn to recognise the sound of each chord. For this reason it's worth revisiting these early exercises even when you've progressed to the later stages.

The chord will be played three times. What you need to do is:

1) Listen to the chord played for the first time— hit pause on your CD player—and have a go at figuring out what chord it is. You can write down your answer on the chart below.

2) Hit play again, listen to the chord for a second time, and then hit pause again. Have another go at working out what the chord is (hopefully you'll be confirming what you thought the first time).

3) Hit play again, but this time play the chord you think it is along with me, and you should hear whether you've got it right or not.

You can fill in your answers in the chart on the opposite page. There are copies of all the charts for the J.U.S.T.I.N. exercises as PDF files on CD2.

Getting Started

Stage 1

Stage 2

Stage 3

Stage 4

Stage 5

Stage 6

Stage 7

Stage 8

Stage 9

Bonus

SSR Test

CD 1 Track
7

Chord Palette: D, A, E

		Attempt 1	Attempt 2	Attempt 3
CHORD	1.			
	2.			
	3.			
	4.			
	5.			

Chord Progression Recognition (CPR)

In this exercise you will hear some chord progressions that you have to figure out by ear. In the SSR exercises you'll work out one chord at a time. In this exercise—and at the same point in the other stages—you'll work out a sequence of chords played one after the other, just like working out the chords for a song. The trick is to pause on each chord and try and figure it out before continuing. At this stage I will be playing each chord for a full bar: four down-strums on each. You only have three chords to choose from, so you should find this easy enough.

CD 1 Track
8

Chord Palette: D, A, E

BAR		1.	2.	3.	4.
EXERCISE	1.				
	2.				
	3.				

REMEMBER to stop the track right after the chord you are trying to identify because... ...The Last Thing You Hear, Stays In Your Ear! Take it slow and don't expect results too quickly. It WILL take some time to develop your listening skills.

If you're not sure, you'll find the answers to this on page 53.

Getting Started

Stage 1

Stage 2

Stage 3

Stage 4

Stage 5

Stage 6

Stage 7

Stage 8

Stage 9

Bonus

 In this first stage we'll keep it nice and simple...

...only **18 minutes** per session.

 Things to remember

Chord Practice

The point of this exercise is to get each note of your chords sounding clear, with no dead notes or buzz, and to train your fingers to go to exactly the right spot.

- Start with a strum, then pick each note individually, and then strum again.
- Don't play any strings that have the X next to them in the chord diagram.
- Try to play the notes with the tips of your fingers.
- Remember that dead-sounding notes or buzzing need to be fixed, and the usual causes are either:
  a) The finger is too far from the fret.
  b) One of your fingers is touching a string that it shouldn't.

Move your fingers around as you pick out the strings until they all sound good and then strum the chord again; as you play the last strum, tell your fingers that this is where you want them to go to next time. It will look a little strange to anyone that is watching you, but it really helps!

One-Minute Changes

The object of this exercise is to get your fingers moving quickly. Although you should be trying to get the fingers in the perfect positions that you have been working on in your chord practice, if they are a little sloppy it is OK, we are working up the speed here! In your practice schedule you should write in the amount of changes that you made in that practice session. Make sure you use your timer, and push yourself to go as fast as possible.

Songs/Chord Sequences

The idea here is just to have fun and dig on the fact that you should now be able to play some of the songs from the songbook, as listed on page 35. Pick one song and work on getting it as smooth as possible. Memorising the chord sequence for the song will certainly help if you are able to. However, I would recommend maybe starting off with some 'made-up' sequences just to get you going. Below are some four-bar chord sequences using D, A and E to try.

Playing chord sequences, or progressions, is a great way to develop your chord changes without the pressure of playing songs. The majority of people enjoy playing songs more, but they are both of great benefit.

Because there is no melody or lyrics to the chord progressions you can concentrate fully on making the changes between the chords as smooth as possible. The aim is not to stop at all, and to keep the timing of the strums perfectly evenly spaced. You are sure to recognise some of the progressions as being from famous songs too. You could even make up your own chord progressions if you want to!

J.U.S.T.I.N. Training

This is really important! Put the work in now and you will reap the benefits later.

 Chord sequences to try: four down-strokes to a bar.

These symbols—‖: :‖—show you that you should repeat the sequence.

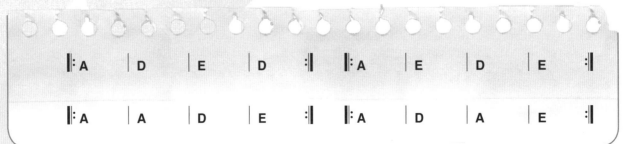

| ‖: A | D | E | D :‖ | ‖: A | E | D | E :‖ |

| ‖: A | A | D | E :‖ | ‖: A | D | A | E :‖ |

[]

justinguitar.com

Getting Started

Stage 1

Stage 2

Stage 3

Stage 4

Stage 5

Stage 6

Stage 7

Stage 8

Stage 9

Bonus

Stage 1 Practice chart (18 minutes)

Start date: _____

Use this chart to monitor your progress each day. There is a PDF of this chart on the CD for you to print out when you run out of space, or if you don't want to write in the book.

Work	Details	Time	M	T	W	T	F	S	S
Chord Practice	D	00:02:00							
	A	00:02:00							
	E	00:02:00							
One-Minute Changes (write in how many changes you did each day)	D to A	00:01:00							
	D to E	00:01:00							
	A to E	00:01:00							
Songs/Chord Sequences (write in details each day)		00:05:00							
J.U.S.T.I.N. Training	Single Sound Recognition	00:02:00							
	Chord Progression Recognition	00:02:00							

When should I move on to Stage 2?

It's very hard for me to define the point at which you should move onto the next stage. You should understand the content of the stage, but many skills will develop over the course as well.

The real answer is to move on when YOU feel ready. However, I know that it can be hard to tell when you feel ready or not! So, here are some suggestions as to what you should have accomplished before moving on:

• You should know all the chords from this stage—D, A and E—from memory.
• You should have them sounding good (if not perfect), with most of the notes sounding out most of the time.

• You should have your One-Minute changes down to at least 20 changes in a minute.
• You should be able to play one or two of the songs from the songbook, even if you have to start and stop a little bit here and there.

Beware of trying to perfect every stage, as that will just lead to a feeling of hopelessness! I'm still trying to perfect simple things, and to be honest, I don't think we ever stop improving, so there is no 'end game'—don't wait until every chord is PERFECT, be happy with good. Perfect will come later! That said, don't try and move on to the next stage if you are sloppy as a wet sandwich!

I hope that helps you decide when to move on!

51

Stage 2

Getting Started

Stage 1

Stage 2

Stage 3

Stage 4

Stage 5

Stage 6

Stage 7

Stage 8

Stage 9

Bonus

 ## Introduction

So, you've have made it to Stage 2. Well done! I hope your fingers are starting to hurt less and you are enjoying playing a couple of songs with your D, A and E chords.

In this stage, we are going to learn three minor chords. Minor chords are no harder to play than major ones; they just sound a little sad.

Again, it is very important that you commit all the chords you learn to memory. If you ever play at a live gig you don't want to have to get your book out to check the chords, and learning a song will be very frustrating if you have to keep looking at a chord box to remember where to put your fingers! So get them locked into your memory as soon as possible.

BC-127

Here is a list of 10 songs—all included in the Justinguitar.com Beginner's Songbook—which you can play using the chords we'll cover in this stage (and that you already know from the previous stage!):

A Girl Like You (Edwyn Collins)

Louie Louie (The Kingsmen)

I'd Rather Go Blind (Etta James)

Natural Mystic (Bob Marley & The Wailers)

St. James Infirmary Blues (Traditional)

All Your Love (I Miss Loving) (John Mayall & The Bluesbreakers)

Twist And Shout (The Beatles)

Peggy Sue (Buddy Holly)

Lay Down Sally (Eric Clapton)

Wild Thing (The Troggs)

Getting Started

Stage 1

Stage 2

Stage 3

Stage 4

Stage 5

Stage 6

Stage 7

Stage 8

Stage 9

Bonus

J.U.S.T.I.N. TEST ANSWERS FOR STAGE 1

THE ANSWERS! NO PEEKING…

SSR.1) A 2) D 3) E 4) D 5) A

CPR:

EXERCISE	BAR:	1.	2.	3.	4.
1.		A	E	A	D
2.		D	A	E	D
3.		E	A	E	D

The Am Chord

Getting Started

Stage 1

Stage 2

Stage 3

Stage 4

Stage 5

Stage 6

Stage 7

Stage 8

Stage 9

Bonus

The A minor (Am) chord sounds kind of sad...

When you see an 'm' after the name of the chord, it means that it is a minor chord. The three chords we looked at in the previous stage are all major chords, but you don't have to say, for instance, 'A Major' every time; major chords are so common that you can just say 'A'.

CD I Track

9 **Am**

You should notice that this first chord is very similar to the E chord that we learnt on page 42, but with the shape placed on different strings.

Subsequently, you should find changing from Am to E pretty easy. Make sure that your 1st finger is not muting the thinnest string when checking each note individually in your practice.

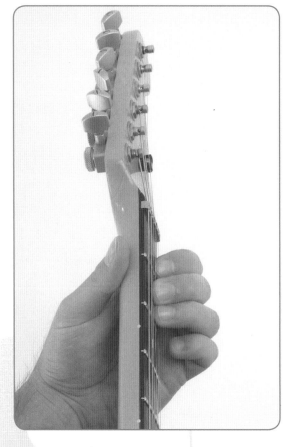

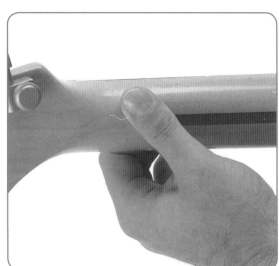

There are only two fingers required for this chord!

CD 1 Track
10

Em

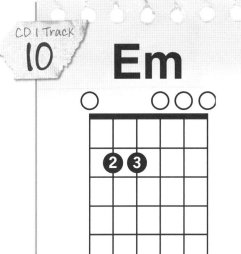

Time to lift a finger! E minor is very easy and you should have no trouble with it. It's just like an E but with one less finger to worry about. There are actually two more options for fingering this chord:

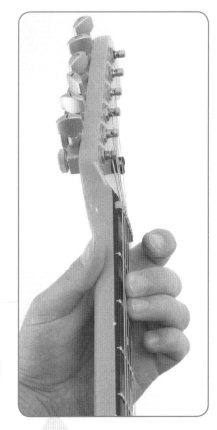

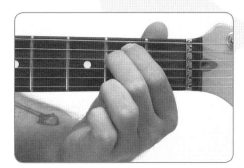

Em

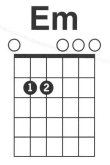

Em

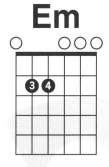

Learn to play this chord with your 2nd and 3rd fingers as shown at the top of the page; later on, you could come back and experiment with using your 1st and 2nd, or 3rd and 4th fingers. You'll eventually find that you'll decide which fingering to use depending upon the song you're playing, and the chords you're playing before or after Em.

Getting Started
Stage 1
Stage 2
Stage 3
Stage 4
Stage 5
Stage 6
Stage 7
Stage 8
Stage 9
Bonus

55

Getting Started

Stage 1

Stage 2

Stage 3

Stage 4

Stage 5

Stage 6

Stage 7

Stage 8

Stage 9

Bonus

A bit of a stretch

D minor can be a little bit of a stretch for a beginner, but you will soon limber up if you keep trying!

CD 1 Track
11

Dm

X X O

Dm requires a different type of hand position to any of the chords so far, but it is not hard to play. Place your fingers as shown, and make sure that your 3rd finger is not muting the first string. Also check that you are only strumming the four strings shown, just like you did for D.

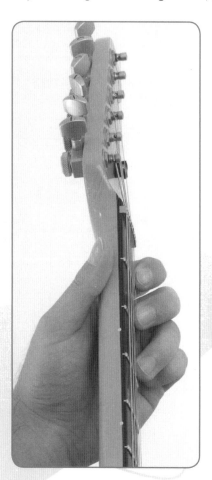

You can use either fingers 1,2 and 3 to play this chord—as shown in the photo and diagram—or use 1, 2 and 4 if you find the stretch too much with your 3rd finger. See what feels good for you. Both fingerings have pros and cons depending on the circumstances.

Some people find it easier to place their fingers down in this order: 3rd finger first, then 2nd and then 1st. This is fine if it works for you, and can help you develop a good stretch. Eventually you will move all your fingers at the same time.

Some people find it a easier to angle the hand a little, pointing your fingers more toward your eyes than at the sky (or you could think of it as if your knuckles are a bit further away from you). This doesn't work for everyone, but experiment with your hand position to see what works well to get all the notes nice and clear.

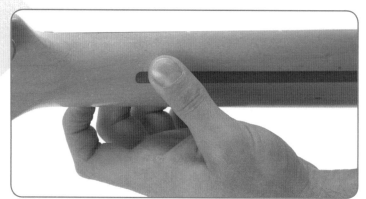

Practise what you can't do, don't practise what you can

If you find one of these changes easy, then substitute it for a change that you find hard. The following changes all have something about them that I think is good to practise, so this is a suggested list to start you off. Eventually you should just work on the ones that you find hardest!

Am to E Try to move the shape as a block without placing one finger at a time.

Am to Dm Work on getting the 3rd finger up near the fret.

A to Dm Anchor the 3rd finger; just slide between the 2nd and 3rd fret.

E to D More work on the anchoring.

Em to D Notice how much easier it was when we had an anchor!

In an ideal world you would do every chord change possible for every chord that you know, but once you get to, say, eight chords (which we will very soon) it would take a long time to do all 28 possible changes (thanks to Francisco for working that out).

It's strange, but you'll probably find that by only working on some chord changes, they all improve. I'm not 100% sure why that is, but my guess is that as you develop your muscle control all the changes get easier.

And, by only working for five minutes you will have time to work on other stuff in your routine which is important too, so don't be tempted to work on all your changes at once unless you have loads of time and can get all your other practice done too!

Most people find changes involving Dm to be the hardest, so don't worry if you're finding it tricky. It's only because Dm has a different kind of stretch for your hand mechanics to get used to, that makes it difficult.

By the way, if you are questioning the effectiveness of the One-Minute Changes idea, have a look on the forum on the website, as there are lots of people who have noticed a significant improvement by sticking at it. And you can too.

You should also be aware that sometimes progress happens in jumps. You'll be stuck on say two changes a minute, and really be struggling, finding it hard and frustrating, and then suddenly you'll jump to 30 changes. What happened? Very often it is tension and anxiety that slow us down, so often when people get fed up and give up trying—and subsequently actually relax—they get heaps better all of a sudden. The moral of the story I guess is to try and stay as relaxed as possible. Take a few deep breaths before you start and stay focused, but not tense (I know it's easier said than done!).

Getting Started

Stage 1

Stage 2

Stage 3

Stage 4

Stage 5

Stage 6

Stage 7

Stage 8

Stage 9

Bonus

 ## Click, click, click, click, click, click, click...

Making friends with the metronome is very important because it will help you develop your sense of rhythm and keep your tempo consistent. If you practise with one, you will find that it helps you develop your 'inner metronome', so that your time improves even when you're not playing to a metronome or 'click'.

It's REALLY important that you can hear the metronome clearly, so use headphones if you can't hear it very well, or leave it resting on top of your guitar where it is close to your ear!

I recommend getting a digital metronome. I do like 'old skool' stuff, but the old 'tick-tock' metronomes are limited in the tempi you can choose from and I think it is a very good idea to have one that can go at every tempo. Really, I guess any metronome will be fine as long as it's digital.

Tempi are measured in BPM (Beats Per Minute); 60bpm equals one click every second.

A very useful feature on some metronomes (like the Korg one) is being able to set an accent. For most of this course you will be playing in 4/4 time, so set the beat to '4', and that way it will accent the first beat of each bar with a different sound so you will always know where '1' is. This is good for

making sure that you put the right number of beats in each bar!

Metronomes are also good at inducing panic in people because they make you get things done at a consistent pace! If you are one of those (many!) people that are quite inconsistent with your One-Minute changes, a small amount of time doing the changes with the metronome might well help you sort that out. Playing along and making sure you hit a chord with every click (or every second click) is a really good way of developing your internal rhythm (and panic control!).

If you don't have the money for a metronome right now, there is a simple metronome built into justinguitar.com (in the left-hand menu) that is completely free! There is a countdown timer as well which you can use to time your practice sessions to make sure that you are spending the right amount of time on the right things.

There are quite a few online metronomes of varying quality and stability that you will find easily with a Google search, but the metronome I use more than any other these days is an iPhone app called Tempo made by Frozen Ape. It works great and has many advanced features that you won't be using right away, but will find very useful as you progress.

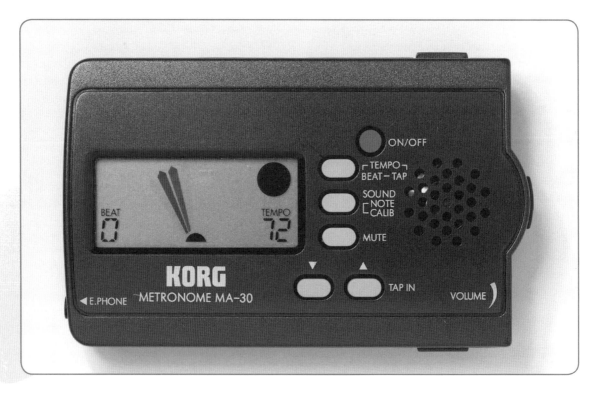

Sounds like a ridiculous thing to teach, right?

Well, I just wanna make sure you get it right... and you'd be amazed how many people say this lesson helped them. Maybe you will too?

Tapping your foot: a checklist

1) If you're sitting down, it's better to tap your left foot (if you're a right-handed player) so that the guitar is not bouncing on your lap.

2) You can also just tap your toes inside your shoes to do it more inconspicuously.

3) Try and get into the habit of tapping your foot whenever you listen to music.

4) Some people nod their head instead; I sometimes step side-to-side... it's all cool if you get in the groove, man!

Exercise

Work on tapping your foot along with a metronome (as covered on the previous page). Start at 60bpm; try and get your foot tapping and do a down-strum along with the metronome click. Really try to start to feel the timing internally, to develop your 'inner metronome'. I know it sounds a little silly but it really is important.

A Good Habit

For any of you that are having timing issues, I always recommend getting into the habit of tapping your foot along to music all the time. Whenever you hear music, train your foot to start tapping along. It doesn't take long (maybe a month or two) for it to become habit. Many students start getting the feeling that their foot is tapping along to a metronome, a recording, or their own playing subconsciously, which is exactly what you want. It's almost like you have to build a little subroutine in your brain that keeps going even while you are thinking about something else!

Getting Started

Stage 1

Stage 2

Stage 3

Stage 4

Stage 5

Stage 6

Stage 7

Stage 8

Stage 9

Bonus

J.U.S.T.I.N. Training Exercises

Getting Started

Stage 1

Stage 2

Stage 3

Stage 4

Stage 5

Stage 6

Stage 7

Stage 8

Stage 9

Bonus

Time to open your ears

In case you're wondering, it does not matter at all if you play acoustic or electric guitar for these exercises. They do sound a little different but the actual notes are the same.

Many people will find some of these exercises harder than others. This is quite normal. It's normal to find this stuff difficult, but as with many things in life, it's the harder things—those that take the most effort—which are the most rewarding. So get stuck in and work hard at them and you will reap the benefit further down the line: working out songs on your own, which is a way cool skill.

Chord Quality Recognition

Now we have to work on working out whether the chords I'm playing are major or minor. I will only be playing either A or Am and you have to work out which is which, so all I want you to write down is 'major' or 'minor'.

CD 1 Track 12

Sound Palette: major or minor

		Attempt 1	Attempt 2	Attempt 3
CHORD	1.			
	2.			
	3.			
	4.			
	5.			

Single Sound Recognition

Now it's time to work out which chord I am playing, just like we did last time. Grab your guitar and get ready. Your chord palette is a little bigger now, so there are six possible chords that I might be playing. Remember to pause after the first play of the chord and then try and figure it out. I play each chord three times, so you can have a few goes. Try and play your guess along with me on the last strum and check that you have it right

CD 1 Track 13

Chord Palette: E, A, D, Em, Am, Dm

		Attempt 1	Attempt 2	Attempt 3
CHORD	1.			
	2.			
	3.			
	4.			
	5.			

Chord Progression Recognition

Just as last time, you have to work out what I play in each of these chord progressions. Remember that our palette is a little larger now—so it will be a little bit harder—but I'm sure you can do it! Again, I'm playing four down-strokes in each bar.

CD 1 Track 14

Chord Palette: E, A, D, Em, Am, Dm

BAR		1.	2.	3.	4.
EXERCISE	1.				
	2.				
	3.				

Answers for all this can be found on page 65!

Getting Started
Stage 1
Stage 2
Stage 3
Stage 4
Stage 5
Stage 6
Stage 7
Stage 8
Stage 9
Bonus

Getting
Started

Stage 1

Stage 2

Stage 3

Stage 4

Stage 5

Stage 6

Stage 7

Stage 8

Stage 9

Bonus

 Introduction

At this stage we'll still keep your practice schedule nice and simple at 22 minutes.

 Things to remember

It is worth quickly reviewing the 'Things to Remember' from Stage 1 on page 50, because all those things will apply for every practice schedule that follows and I've decided not to repeat them all each time. So give them a quick scan before you do your practice until all the tips become instinctive. Don't forget, there's a copy of the practice chart opposite as a PDF file on CD2.

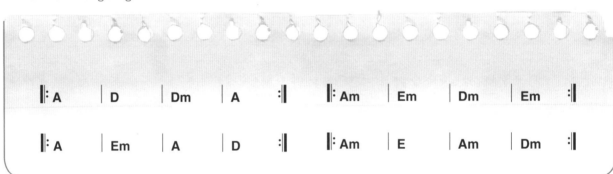 Chord sequences to try

Below are a few common four-bar chord sequences you might like to try out, but again, do try and make up some of your own too. Creating your own sequences will help you learn to listen closely to the ways chords interact and will be very useful later when it comes to working out songs on your own or writing songs.

‖: A | D | Dm | A :‖   ‖: Am | Em | Dm | Em :‖

‖: A | Em | A | D :‖   ‖: Am | E | Am | Dm :‖

Stage 2 Practice chart (22 minutes)

Start date: _____

Work	Details	Time	M	T	W	T	F	S	S
Chord Practice	Am	00:02:00							
	Em	00:02:00							
	Dm	00:02:00							
One-Minute Changes (write in how many changes you did each day)	Am to E	00:01:00							
	Am to Dm	00:01:00							
	A to Dm	00:01:00							
	E to D	00:01:00							
	Em to D	00:01:00							
Songs/Chord Sequences (write in details each day)		00:05:00							
J.U.S.T.I.N. Training	Chord Quality Recognition	00:02:00							
	Single Sound Recognition	00:02:00							
	Chord Progression Recognition	00:02:00							

DON'T FORGET: Tap your foot along whenever you can!

When should I move on to Stage 3?

I'm sure you are wondering if you are ready to move on. As I said at the end of Stage 1, there is no hard and fast answer, but a rough guide is:

- You should know all the chords from this stage from memory as well as the chords from the previous stage.
- You should have them sounding reasonable (if not perfect), with most of the notes coming out most of the time!

- You should have your One-Minute changes down to at least 30 changes in a minute.
- You should be able to play one or two more songs from the songbook—perhaps not perfectly—but be able to kind of play it through, some stops and stutters allowed.
- You should be able to tap your foot along with a metronome consistently (at a medium tempo, say 80bpm)

Getting Started

Stage 1

Stage 2

Stage 3

Stage 4

Stage 5

Stage 6

Stage 7

Stage 8

Stage 9

Bonus

Stage 3

Getting Started

Stage 1

Stage 2

Stage 3

Stage 4

Stage 5

Stage 6

Stage 7

Stage 8

Stage 9

Bonus

 Welcome to Stage 3!

The next two chords we will learn are a little stretchier than the ones we've looked at previously. Some people find them easy, but others really struggle, so don't worry if you don't get them right away. It's O.K. to move your fingers to the right place with your strumming hand if they won't go there by themselves; sometimes it's just that you need to develop a little more flexibility in your fingers.

I'm not sure if it really helped, but when I was learning and struggling with the G chord I used to stretch my fretting hand fingers apart with my strumming hand—kind of stretching out the webbing—you might like to try that if your fingers are feeling really tight and you are having trouble reaching for the chords.

We'll look at a basic finger exercise in this stage as well which can help with stretching and if you really want to work this area there is another finger stretching exercise on my website (in the Technique area, TE-007) which you might find helpful too.

BC-137

Here is a list of 10 songs—all included in the Justinguitar.com Beginner's Songbook—which you can play using the chords you'll know by the end of this stage:

Hey Joe (The Jimi Hendrix Experience)

Knockin' On Heavens Door (Bob Dylan)

Hey Ya! (Outkast)

Brown Eyed Girl (Van Morrison)

Yellow Submarine (The Beatles)

Mr. Tambourine Man (The Byrds)

How To Save A Life (The Fray)

What's Up? (4 Non Blondes)

This Year's Love (David Gray)

Working Class Hero (John Lennon)

J.U.S.T.I.N. TEST ANSWERS FOR STAGE 2

THE ANSWERS! NO PEEKING...
COR: 1) maj 2) min 3) maj 4) maj 5) min
SSR: 1) Am 2) E 3) Dm 4) A 5) D

CPR:

BAR	1.	2.	3.	4.
1.	Am	E	Am	Dm
2.	D	A	Am	E
3.	Dm	D	Dm	A

Sidebar tabs: Getting Started, Stage 1, Stage 2, Stage 3, Stage 4, Stage 5, Stage 6, Stage 7, Stage 8, Stage 9, Bonus

Getting Started

Stage 1

Stage 2

Stage 3

Stage 4

Stage 5

Stage 6

Stage 7

Stage 8

Stage 9

Bonus

Now it's time to have a go at the big 2/3 stretch!

The G Chord can be quite a challenge for some people, but it's a very commonly-used chord, so you need to learn it. If it seems tough, just stick with it, you'll get it as your fingers limber up!

CD 1 Track
15

G

Try not to force your 1st and 2nd fingers apart.

I had many problems with G when I was first learning. Take your time, stretch the fingers, practise it often, and soon the stretch will feel easy. Make sure you are checking that all the notes are ringing out clearly.

There are a few alternative fingerings for this G chord; this is the one that I think is best to start with. However, if you have learnt a different one, stick with that for now. I will be going through some of the other fingerings at a later stage.

So, dig deep and get this one sounding good. I don't want to see any 'my hands are too small' posts on the forum! Maybe some of you have old injuries, broken or bent fingers, and they may well hinder you a little, but I've seen all kinds of people with all kinds of problems and there is one cure for them all: practice and perseverance! You might have to adapt things a little if you have a serious injury, but it would have to be severe to have to change the fingering or shape.

It's tough for most folk when they start (like it was for me) but it just takes a little grit and hard work and in no time you'll be wondering how you ever had a problem with it at all!

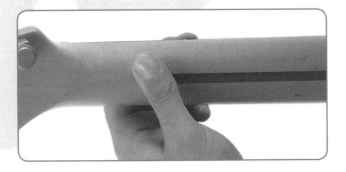

This chord can also be quite a challenge...

This one is a bit of stretch for some hands, but it is a very commonly-used chord, and again, it just takes practice to get right. Those of you with large fingers might think this one is impossible when you start, but it will work, it's just going to take you a bit of time to place your first finger just right. I have seen quite a few private students over the years with short fat fingers playing this chord perfectly, and so I know it just takes practice!

CD 1 Track
16

C

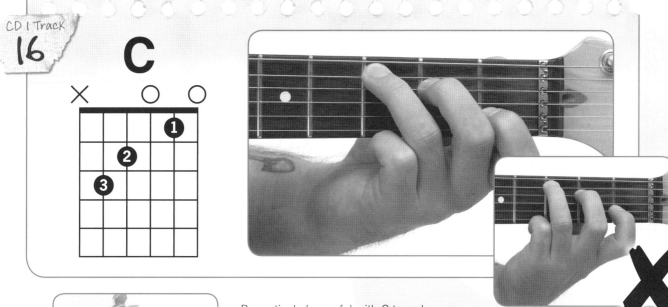

Be particularly careful with C to make sure that you get all the notes clear. Strum, pick out and strum again. The 3rd finger will often mute the D (fourth) string, so watch out for that!

Don't get your fingers too 'square', as it won't feel comfortable.

A couple of tips if you are really struggling: Try pointing your thumb away from your face, and place it further toward the nut, toward the top of the neck (NOT over the top of the neck), probably about opposite your first finger. This should let your fingers be at a little more of an angle and help them get the stretch, as shown above.

Because everyone has different shaped hands and lengths of fingers, the C chord always looks a little different for different people. Some people have their fingers more or less angled, and there is a huge variation in thumb placement between different people. The trick here is to find the method that is best for you that keeps all the notes clear and keeps the thumb behind the neck (you can bring it over later but I strongly discourage beginners from doing this!).

Stretching between the 2nd and 3rd fingers just does not work: our hands didn't evolve to do that, it's not practical, so avoid trying to do it.

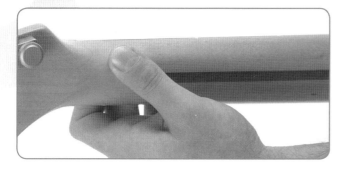

Getting Started

Stage 1

Stage 2

Stage 3

Stage 4

Stage 5

Stage 6

Stage 7

Stage 8

Stage 9

Bonus

The Names Of The Open Strings

Getting Started

Stage 1

Stage 2

Stage 3

Stage 4

Stage 5

Stage 6

Stage 7

Stage 8

Stage 9

Bonus

It's a very useful thing to know the note names of the open strings on your guitar.

They are often used to describe finger placement (e.g., "put your 1st finger in the 2nd fret of the A string"), and are also useful for tuning your guitar to another instrument (like a piano). You need to know this when you buy a replacement string for your guitar (e.g., "can I please have a D string") and will help you learn the names of the notes that you are playing. Knowing the names of the strings will also help you use a guitar tuner.

So, it's well worth putting the time in on this one, and we will be developing this more in a latter stage when we learn all the notes in the open position and the notes that make up our chords!

So, what are the notes?

First string: E (the thinnest)

Second string: B

Third string: G

Fourth string: D

Fifth string: A

Sixth string: E (the thickest)

One of the best ways to remember the note names is to make up sayings:

From Thick to Thin:

• Eddie Ate Dynamite, Good Bye Eddie!
• Easter Angels Don't Give Broken Eggs

From Thin to Thick:

• Easter Bunny Gets Drunk After Easter
• Every Boy Gets Dizzy Around Elle

Try making up your own; you don't have to use one of mine! Just make sure you remember it!

Get your timer out and get your fingers moving faster

So here we are for more One-Minute Changes, and these ones are going to be a little trickier thanks to our new friends G and C, which are often going to require all the fingers to come off and be replaced. Many people find the change from C to G to be the hardest change at this stage—I sure found that one hard when I was first learning—but it just takes practice.

C to Am Just move your 3rd finger without letting the others lift up!

C to A Keep your 2nd finger down as an anchor.

C to G All change! The hardest change so far, but a very common chord change, so you have to work at it.

G to E All change! Another common change.

G to D All change! Another common change.

Just so you know, it's fine to experiment with finger placement order for One-Minute Changes; you don't have to always start with the 1st finger. In fact, this can be a good thing to do. In a couple of stages time we're going to be putting down all the fingers at once, so getting used to a different finger order and the control that requires can be good mental exercise.

The most common changes in finger order placement are to start the C Chord with the third finger (which helps with the stretch between 3 and 2). Some people also like to put the third finger down first for a G (which I don't get really, but if it works for them...).

To help get your numbers up it can help to do a few warm up changes before you get going, just to get the finger movements in the 'now' part of your brain and to get the muscle memory working.

Remember too that you won't be alone if you are finding these new chords hard, in particular changes using the G and the C. This is normal; it's just going to take a little practice like everything else. So don't get down about it. Enjoy the journey!

It is worth noting that I still do this exercise when I have trouble with new chords with odd shapes or stretches, and it really helps. I warm up with a few really slow changes, make sure that I've got my fingers in a good position and then go for it for a minute. After a few sets of changes I've usually cracked the new chords.

Getting Started

Stage 1

Stage 2

Stage 3

Stage 4

Stage 5

Stage 6

Stage 7

Stage 8

Stage 9

Bonus

Basic Finger Workout

Getting Started

Stage 1

Stage 2

Stage 3

Stage 4

Stage 5

Stage 6

Stage 7

Stage 8

Stage 9

Bonus

Spread 'em!

This very basic exercise will help you develop a bit of strength and independence in your fingers. Although exercises like this can be a little boring, they help you develop your physical skills faster and will get you playing your songs better, so they are well worth the effort.

We are going to be starting around the 5th fret with our 1st finger on the 5th fret of the thickest string. We are going to play that note, and then we are going to put our second finger down on the 6th fret of the same string, then our 3rd finger on the seventh fret of the same string and then reaching up with the little finger up into the 8th fret. The thing that we should be noticing here is that each finger is right up next to its respective fret; it's easy for the 3rd and 4th fingers to fall next to each other instead of being in the right place. The other thing that I want you to notice is that when the little finger is down all the other fingers should stay down in the right place. So, we are really after keeping our fingers nicely locked down; you should feel some stretch. Play this all using down-picks. Here's what your hand should look like when you've got all four fingers down, with the fingers stretched out across the frets. See how the fingers are pressed right up against the frets. This exercise is shown in tab here; if tab is new for you, check the guide on page 31.

CD 1 Track
17

Play the sixth string:

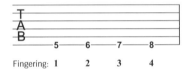

Fingering: 1   2   3   4

And then onto the fifth string:

1   2   3   4

The fourth string:

1   2   3   4

Third string:

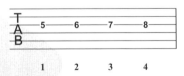

1   2   3   4

Second string:

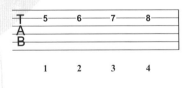

1   2   3   4

And onto the thinnest string:

1   2   3   4

CD 1 Track
18

Here's the whole exercise:

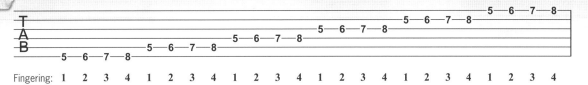

Fingering: 1 2 3 4 1 2 3 4 1 2 3 4 1 2 3 4 1 2 3 4 1 2 3 4

Then when we go back in the other direction we still go up each string, starting with the 1st finger:

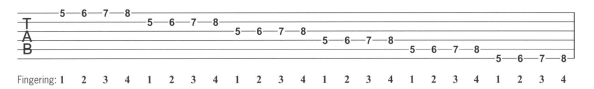

Fingering: 1 2 3 4 1 2 3 4 1 2 3 4 1 2 3 4 1 2 3 4 1 2 3 4

If you find this too easy, you can move your fingers further down the neck (towards the nut), where the frets are further apart, until you get down to the 1st fret.

Make sure that you:

Hold the fingers down as you go

When you put down your little finger, make sure that all your fingers are still pressing down in the correct frets. This is what helps you develop the stretch between the fingers, which makes them more agile. Holding them down also works the muscles, making your fingers stronger.

Use your fingertips

Don't let the fingers fall flat. Keep the fingers slightly rounded and make sure that the tip of your finger is holding down the strings. This helps you develop correct technique and also toughens up the ends of your fingers. People with small little fingers (like me!) struggle to keep their little finger on the tip without touching the other strings when playing the thickest string. It will just take a little more work than those lucky long-fingered people. Don't stress if you don't get it right away; it just takes a bit of work. If you have normal or long little finger you should find it kind of lays out a little and is more rounded than mine looks; it's just because I have a little stump that it looks parallel to the other fingers!

Five minutes per day will be enough

Don't go over the top and practise this too much or you might hurt yourself! Five minutes is enough to get a bit of a workout without any straining.

Relax into your posture

If you are having to contort your arm and wrist into all sorts of strange positions to get this right, then try and hold your hand in position and relax your body and arm (while keeping your hand in as good a position as you can). Part of the exercise is for you to learn how to use your body comfortably to make these shapes and play these notes. Everyone is a little different so we all have to find our own way here a bit!

By the way, here's my view of finger exercise machines: a waste of time, money and energy. Work the muscles out by playing guitar, it's more fun and you will learn other stuff too! I've heard a few students say that they found some benefit from these kinds of devices, but I'm sure that they would have got the same or more benefit doing an exercise like this. Maybe those strange people who live near a park yet prefer to run on a treadmill like using them, I guess...

Do be careful not to hurt yourself! Take it easy, relax and stretch out, you'll get it in no time. Short, simple exercises like this can make a big difference.

Getting Started
Stage 1
Stage 2
Stage 3
Stage 4
Stage 5
Stage 6
Stage 7
Stage 8
Stage 9
Bonus

Really Useful Strumming Techniques (R.U.S.T.)

R.U.S.T. stands for 'Really Useful Strumming Techniques'. As part of this beginner's course I will be showing you some patterns to get you started on rhythm guitar. At the end of this book, if you want to check out more rhythm lessons in greater detail you might want to check out my Really Useful Strumming Techniques DVD.

This is as basic as it gets, but it is very important that you learn to play this pattern well, because pretty much all rhythm patterns are based on this simple pattern. On page 46 (BC-116), we looked at this strumming pattern:

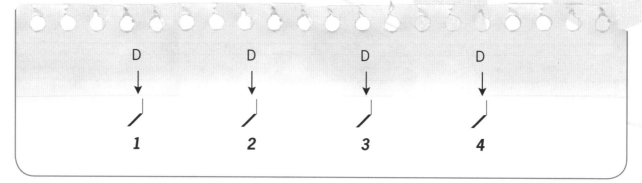

The next concept that I want to introduce is that of an 'and'. Now, we previously mentioned that in a bar we have four beats. So we count "one, two, three, four", and these four are all down-strums.

Now, this is the big secret for rhythm guitar: you have to keep your hand moving evenly all of the time. As your hand is moving down on the beat every time, it means that your hand will be moving

up in between every beat. So what we are going to introduce now is adding one up-strum to our regular rhythm. If we want to add something in between those beats this is where we introduce a thing called the 'and'. So normally when counting music you would have "one and two and three and four and", the 'ands' falling exactly half way between the numbers, or beats.

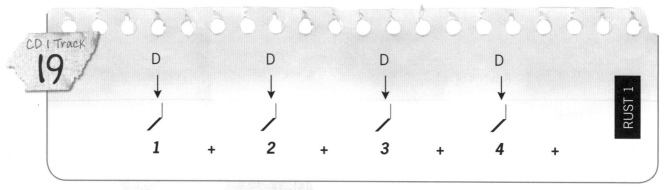

Now, we'll add an up-strum on the 'and' of '3':

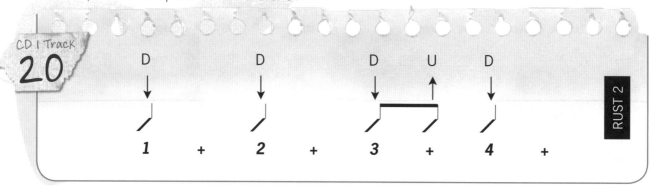

justinguitar.com

Getting Started

Stage 1

Stage 2

Stage 3

Stage 4

Stage 5

Stage 6

Stage 7

Stage 8

Stage 9

Bonus

The aim here is to repeat this pattern until it becomes instinctive. You should aim to be able to put the up-strum in the right place without thinking about it at all. To do that you just need to practise it over and over again! It is very important to do this repetition as much as you can. We will be developing these patterns more in coming stages, but it's better to be able to play a few strumming patterns very well, than playing lots of patterns badly!

The key thing here is to make sure that those four down-strums stay even. Play with a metronome; the up-strum will fall between the metronome clicks. Try setting your metronome at between 60 and 100 bpm. Some people find it harder to play very slow (60bpm) and others when it is faster (over 100bpm) so start with what is easy for you, and slowly work toward what you find hardest. In the end you want to be able to play this and every other pattern you know at a range of tempi.

Note as well that it's fine if the up-strum just hits the first three or four strings. You don't need to strum them all; in fact, it's better if you don't in this example. Once you are comfortable playing these patterns on one chord, have a go at using this pattern while using two chords that you find easy to change between:

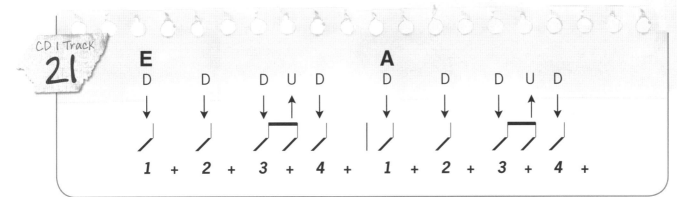

CD 1 Track 21

YOU MUST NOT STOP THE STRUMMING. If you can't do your chord changes fast enough to keep strumming then don't try and apply this to a song yet. In the next stage I will help you out more by teaching you to 'force' the changes (page 85) but the big deal here is: DO NOT STOP STRUMMING. Don't expect it to be easy either. Changing chords while strumming is going to take some practice, so be prepared to dig in.

Probably the most important thing to learn about strumming is to just keep going. As soon as you stop, you are waving a big flag that tells everyone you just screwed up. Even non-musicians will know right away that something is wrong when the rhythm stops, but many people will never notice a wrong or slightly wrong chord.

The other very important factor is to RELAX. Make sure you keep your arm as relaxed as possible. Of course, it needs a little tension to move and hold the pick, but otherwise keep your whole body as relaxed as possible and learn to let the music flow, rather than forcing it. I know it can be hard to relax when you struggle with something, and it's ironic that sometimes the tension is causing the problem... so just do your best and try and stay as relaxed as possible.

I've noticed on the forum that a few people were worried about the exact angle of the strum over the strings. This is not important at this stage. It changes depending upon what you are doing, so beware of analysis paralysis! Don't think yourself into a mental block. At these early stages (especially if you follow my advice) you won't develop any bad habits that can't be fixed a little later.

If you are struggling with anything, then SLOW DOWN. This is the key thing for all guitar practice. When something is hard, slow down, get it right and then speed up. I really can't emphasize this enough: slow makes good.

Getting Started

Stage 1

Stage 2

Stage 3

Stage 4

Stage 5

Stage 6

Stage 7

Stage 8

Stage 9

Bonus

Chord Quality Recognition

In this test, we are still working out if chords are major or minor. I will be playing either D or Dm and you have to work out if the chord played is major or minor. Try and listen for a 'happy' (major) or 'sad' (minor) chord. Like everything else, it's going to take practice, but you can work on this on your own as well. Play D and D minor and listen closely to the difference between the two. Try this with A and A minor too. Listen for the feeling in the chord. After a while it should be very obvious!

CD 1 Track
22

Sound Palette: major or minor

CHORD		Attempt 1	Attempt 2	Attempt 3
	1.			
	2.			
	3.			
	4.			
	5.			

Single Sound Recognition

Now it gets a little harder because our palette is a bit bigger—but you can do it—just remember to pause right after I play the chord. Then start playing your guitar and figure out what chord I played. This is a big deal and will really help you start working out songs on your own, because it's the same process. It's a really cool skill to develop and it's nowhere near as hard as you might think.

CD 1 Track 23

Chord Palette: E, A, D, Em, Am, Dm, G, C

CHORD		Attempt 1	Attempt 2	Attempt 3
	1.			
	2.			
	3.			
	4.			
	5.			

Chord Progression Recognition

Now we're working more on working out our chord progressions, the same as we have been working on already; still just one chord per bar, with four strums on each. Remember you will pause the track after the chord you are working on. Don't try and listen to the whole progression and work it out. That is really hard. Just take it one chord at a time, write them down and then once you got it, try and play along and check that it's right. Then—and only then—should you check your answers.

CD 1 Track 24

Chord Palette: E, A, D, Em, Am, Dm, G, C

BAR		1.	2.	3.	4.
EXERCISE	1.				
	2.				
	3.				

Only look at the answers on page 79 if you really have to!

At this stage we're up to a 30-minute workout.

If you find this too much, then try breaking it into two 15-minute practice sessions on alternate days.

 Things to remember

Finger Workout

Please remember that this exercise is about developing your finger strength and independence and stretch, so please don't try and play this exercise fast, as there's no point!

Rhythm Guitar Practice

Spend your time playing the pattern over and over again; don't try and add the strumming patterns to songs yet. That will be coming soon, and you will do it LOADS better if you follow my advice here and work on the patterns independently before you apply them.

Chord sequences to try

‖: G	C	D	Em :‖		‖: Am	Am	E	E
						C	C	D	E :‖

‖: C	G	Am	Dm :‖

‖: C	G	D	A		‖: G	D	C	C
E	E	E	E :‖		G	D	Am	Am :‖

Stage 3 Practice chart (30 minutes)

Start date: _____

Work	Details	Time	M	T	W	T	F	S	S
Finger Workout		00:05:00							
Chord Practice	G	00:02:00							
	C	00:02:00							
One-Minute Changes (write in how many changes you did each day)	C to Am	00:01:00							
	C to A	00:01:00							
	C to G	00:01:00							
	G to E	00:01:00							
	G to D	00:01:00							
Rhythm Guitar	Repetition	00:05:00							
Songs/Chord Sequences (write in details each day)		00:05:00							
J.U.S.T.I.N. Training	Chord Quality Recognition	00:02:00							
	Single Sound Recognition	00:02:00							
	Chord Progression Recognition	00:02:00							

When should I move on to Stage 4?

Part of the learning process here is for you develop as a student and learn to judge when it's time to move on. If you have an 'in the flesh' teacher then you have to rely on their judgement to know when it's time to move forward, but be aware that teachers naturally feel guilty if they are not giving out new material and so will sometimes rush a student onto new things even if they would probably be better off staying and perfecting the previous week's work!

So, when to move on? When you feel like you have the material under your fingers and it's going O.K. Don't be looking for perfection, just that you feel you are making progress and you are ready for new material. It's a really good idea to develop this as a feeling (rather than making it too academic), and so from now on you will have to call it yourself!

Getting Started
Stage 1
Stage 2
Stage 3
Stage 4
Stage 5
Stage 6
Stage 7
Stage 8
Stage 9
Bonus

Stage 4

Getting Started

Stage 1

Stage 2

Stage 3

Stage 4

Stage 5

Stage 6

Stage 7

Stage 8

Stage 9

Bonus

 Stage 4 already!

The eight chords you have learned already are the most important to work on, so really make sure you have those changes good and all the grips memorised before you spend time looking at the new chords in this stage. Don't expect anything to be perfect yet, because you've not been playing long. I want you to be aware that the chords we're learning in this stage are very useful, and sound cool, but they are used a lot less often than our A, D, E, G, C, Am, Em and Dm grips.

In this stage we're going to look at G7, C7 and B7 chords, which have a very interesting sound and can add a wonderful texture when used in the right place.

Note that 'extended' chords (those with a bigger name than just major or minor) can be simplified down to a more basic major or minor form. For example, if you see a G7 and can't remember how to play it, you could just play a G. If you saw an A7b9 you could play an A. An Emin9 can be simplified to Em. But it doesn't work the other way; so if you see a B chord, you can't assume it's O.K. to play a B7. You can try it, but listen carefully. It will sound great sometimes but not others… hence one of my most important rules about music: if it sounds good, it is good.

BC-147

Here is a list of 10 songs—all included in the Justinguitar.com Beginner's Songbook—which you'll be able to play using the chords we'll have covered by the end of this stage:

Killing Me Softly With His Song (Roberta Flack)

(Sittin' On) The Dock Of The Bay (Otis Redding)

...Baby One More Time (Britney Spears)

Save Tonight (Eagle-Eye Cherry)

Celebrity (Brad Paisley)

Back To December (Taylor Swift)

Black (Pearl Jam)

Little Lion Man (Mumford & Sons)

Live Forever (Oasis)

I Want To Hold Your Hand (The Beatles)

Getting Started

Stage 1

Stage 2

Stage 3

Stage 4

Stage 5

Stage 6

Stage 7

Stage 8

Stage 9

Bonus

J.U.S.T.I.N. TEST ANSWERS FOR STAGE 3

THE ANSWERS! NO PEEKING...

CQR: 1) min 2) min 3) maj 4) min 5) maj

SSR: 1) G 2) C 3) Am 4) E 5) Dm

CPR:

BAR:	1.	2.	3.	4.
EXERCISE 1.	C	G	D	C
2.	Am	A	E	D	E
3.	E	Am	C	G	E

79

Getting Started

Stage 1

Stage 2

Stage 3

Stage 4

Stage 5

Stage 6

Stage 7

Stage 8

Stage 9

Bonus

 Now it's time to stretch out those fingers with some 7 chords.

Adding a 7th does not necessarily make a chord harder to play than regular major or minor chords, but you might find them a little tricky simply because you'll be using your little finger. 7 Chords (otherwise known as 7th or dominant 7th chords) have a very distinct sound and are used a lot in Blues, Folk and Country.

G7

This is a bit of a finger stretcher. It's a bit like a wider version of C, but it won't be difficult after a little practice. It sounds really cool when you're playing blues.

Start with your 1st finger and then stretch the other two fingers across. Keep it easy by remembering to keep your fingers round (like you are holding a ball) and use the tips of your fingers, not the flats.

CD 1 Track **25**

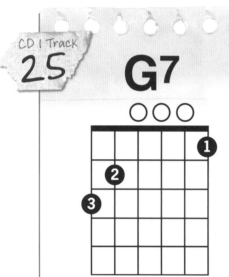

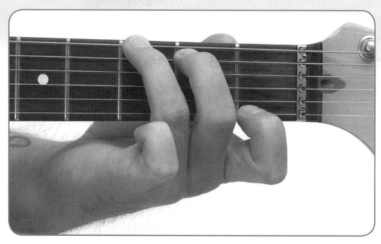

In this photo, I've moved my little finger out of the way so you can see where your other fingers should be...

...and this one shows where your little finger will naturally sit when you play the chord; be careful not to let it touch any of the strings.

C7

To play this chord, start with a regular C chord, and then add your little finger. When you are O.K. with that, try to mute the sixth string with the tip of your 3rd finger. It will make the chord sound better, because the low E makes the chord sound muddy, and also makes more room under your finger to try and let the note on the fourth string ring out clearly.

B7

B7 is a chord you will often come across. I didn't have a hard time with this one when I was learning, but many people do! It can be hard to get all the notes ringing out clearly. The little finger has to press hard as well, and some people find that finger to be weak because it's not been used much up to this point. It could get sore quicker than your other fingers, because the skin hasn't toughened up yet. Check that the tip of your 2nd finger is muting the sixth string and that the second string is ringing out clearly, and is not touched by the 3rd or 4th fingers. That is the hardest bit to get right, for sure. As you might guess, the solution is practice!

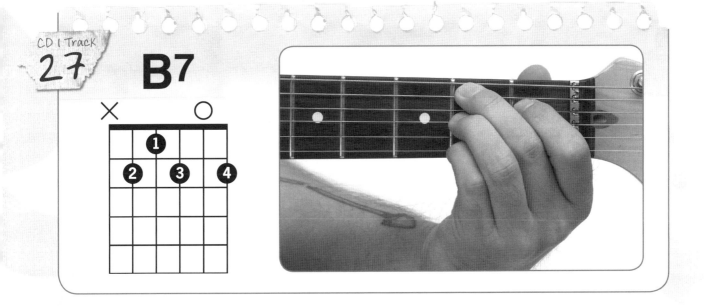

Getting Started

Stage 1

Stage 2

Stage 3

Stage 4

Stage 5

Stage 6

Stage 7

Stage 8

Stage 9

Bonus

A great way around F

Now you have done some hard stretches and given your little finger some punishment, I'll show you a little cheat for the F Chord which sounds great and is really useful!

CD I Track
28 **Fmaj7**

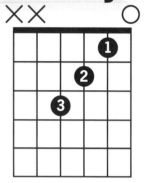

The big F chord is a little nasty so until we learn that in Stage 6 (page 108) I want you to check out this chord, which is easy to play and SOMETIMES sounds good as a substitute for F.

You MUST listen if you are going to try and substitute this one for a big F chord. Sometimes you can replace a regular F with this chord, sometimes you can't. There is theory behind it, but it's too complicated to go into now and it is more important to use your ears to hear if it sounds good or not. If it sounds good, it is good!

It will always work as a substitute for F if your 1st finger lays a bit flat and mutes the thinnest string, because then you are playing a regular F (the open E string is what makes this chord a 'Major' 7th).

If you've got the hang of the chord shown above, you could also try this shape, which brings your little finger into play as well.

Fmaj7

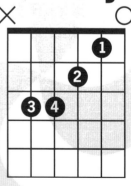

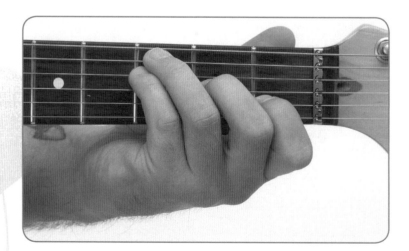

Holding down more than one string with the same finger!

CD 1 Track
29

A

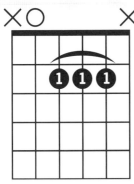

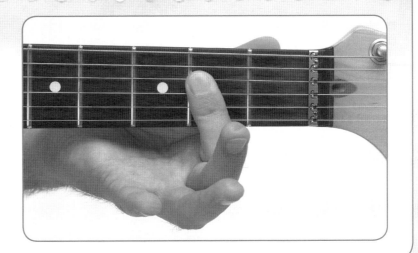

We already learnt to play the A chord on page 40, but there is another way to play it that many people find easier. This is the way that I play A most of the time, especially when playing rock music on electric guitar.

What we have done is taken away the note on the thinnest string (the open E) and we can play all the notes with your 1st finger. This is called using a barre.

It's important to lift your 1st finger a little so that the thinnest string is muted; touching it very lightly will stop it ringing out. If you barre the thinnest string too, you will be playing The 'Elvis' chord: an A6!

If you wanted to try and let the thin open E string ring out, it would not sound bad, but it's hard to do and so not worth it! Sometimes it just sounds better not to have the thin string ringing out. I know it doesn't seem logical, but sometimes it just sounds better without that extra note.

There are a few people who play this with fingers other than their 1st finger, but I really don't recommend it. If it still sounds the same I guess it's OK, but it might make chord changes to and from A a lot harder. Using your

1st finger keeps the others free for adding in other cool stuff later on, like sus chords and blues riffs. Also, using a part barre with your 1st finger and another finger is a bad idea. I strongly advise using just your 1st finger.

Playing this way is going to take some practice, and some people choose to leave out this chord, but I think it's a good idea to learn this one too. It will help get your fingers strong for the dreaded F chord in Stage 6 (page 108).

Make sure that you don't play that thickest string, or the chord will sound muddy. You might find your thumb poking up over the neck. If this is happening it is fine. You could actually let it drop down and mute the thickest string if you like, which is a very useful skill but not an important thing to be doing at this stage.

It's definitely OK to keep working on the original way of playing A, as you will use them both depending on the circumstance. I must admit that it is rare these days that I play the A Chord with three fingers, but it does happen from time to time, and when learning beginner songs it is very useful to have both chord shapes as an option.

Like this: notice the forward knuckle position.

Not like this: pulling your hand back.

This is what it'll look like.

Getting Started

Stage 1

Stage 2

Stage 3

Stage 4

Stage 5

Stage 6

Stage 7

Stage 8

Stage 9

Bonus

Getting Started

Stage 1

Stage 2

Stage 3

Stage 4

Stage 5

Stage 6

Stage 7

Stage 8

Stage 9

Bonus

Them chords they keep a-changin'...

...and we had a whole heap of new chords in this stage, so you have some work to do! By this stage, you should be identifying the changes that you need to work on alongside my suggestions.

C to G7 Starting with C, stretch your fingers out to play G7

C7 to Fmaj7 Keep 1st finger down as an anchor.

E to B7 2nd finger anchor for this chord change.

? to ? (most people find G to C is good to work on)

Some other good suggestions:

C7 to G7

This is a tough one for many people! Getting the little finger to behave can be tricky.
Do it slow a few times before you start and make sure your fingers know where they are going.

D to A (mini barre)
These chords are often found together in songs, so they are a good couple!

E7 to A (mini barre) These are another commonly found couple.

Fmaj7 to A (mini barre) Just because it's kind of tricky!

Remember that working on one change helps most of the others too, so don't stress out about trying to do every possible chord change because there are simply too many, and you are better off putting time into playing songs too.

Forcing The Changes

Use the force!

This technique can be a little hard to get your head around but I have seen this make a huge difference to many people's playing, and hopefully it will be a big help to you, too!

The idea of this exercise is simple. Force yourself to make chord changes faster by not allowing yourself to stop strumming. The benefit is immediate, because if you can keep your strumming going then it will sound cooler and more like a 'proper' song.

Start by playing a chord sequence that you are familiar with—maybe one from page 50—strumming nice and simple, four down-strums to the bar.

If you're having difficulty changing between any of the chords, try and keep strumming in time—even if you are hitting the open strings—don't stop strumming the even four down-strums per bar pattern.

What you will find is that the fretting hand will not want to let the side down, and that your chord changes will actually get faster. I know it sounds a bit strange, but it works really well.

Don't worry if you fluff the chord up a little; just keep strumming. Force your fingers to make the changes. If a finger goes down on a wrong string, just keep playing, and move it while you continue to strum.

A good tip is to use a metronome and strum along with that, it will force you to keep in time, because many people slow down for difficult bits and strum faster in the easy bits, and that just sounds terrible.

So, try it now with a basic chord sequence that you are comfortable with. Put a metronome on and strum your four down strums on each chord and DON"T STOP—even if the chord goes wrong and you don't get all your fingers down in time—DON'T STOP. Just keep going. DON'T STOP!

Rhythm is a really important thing for us humans, and people will notice when the rhythm stops, but they won't notice if a few notes are missing from your chord.

I can't stress the importance of this enough. It's hard to explain in text, but you have to make sure you don't stop strumming even if the chord changes are not fast enough. If it's a real disaster then slow the metronome down. If you are able to do your One-Minute Changes at 60 a minute then setting your metronome at 60bpm should not create too many problems. If you are struggling it's probably due to the panic of being forced to make your changes fast and smooth, and this is the perfect exercise to sort this out!!

The exercise is important because you need to be able to keep a consistent rhythm before you add in more complex strumming patterns.

It might seems strange at first to do it this way but I've seen it help hundreds of students and read that it's helped thousands more online!

Getting Started

Stage 1

Stage 2

Stage 3

Stage 4

Stage 5

Stage 6

Stage 7

Stage 8

Stage 9

Bonus

Getting Started

Stage 1

Stage 2

Stage 3

Stage 4

Stage 5

Stage 6

Stage 7

Stage 8

Stage 9

Bonus

Using some more eighth notes to make a cool pattern.

Now we are going to bring in some more eighth notes to make two very common patterns.

This first pattern adds an up-strum on the 'and' of both '3' and '4':

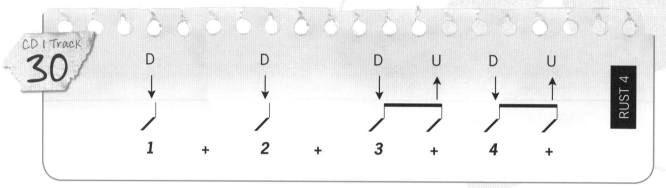

CD 1 Track **30**

D		D		D	U	D	U
1	+	2	+	3	+	4	+

RUST 4

One very common thing that happens in the real world is that when you are changing chords, you'll actually end up playing the open strings of the guitar on the final up-strum of the bar, rather than holding the last chord right to the end. Don't be afraid of it—it's O.K.—once you know this is happening you'll hear it on many hit records and great songs and it doesn't make them sound bad at all.

I can choose when I do it or when I don't, but it's a great help for a beginner to have that little extra time to make the chord changes (not that we will be joining the chord sequences and the strumming patterns just yet!).

I know you might think that sometimes it's not going to sound good, and you would be right. Sometimes it sounds great and sometimes it doesn't. You have to use your ears (again!). If it sounds good, it is good.

This is another important, commonly-used pattern: up-strums on the 'and' after '2' and '3'. We will be developing this pattern soon, so make sure that you give this plenty of practice. Really aim to make it feel natural and easy, so you don't have to think about it. Repetition will make it work for you!

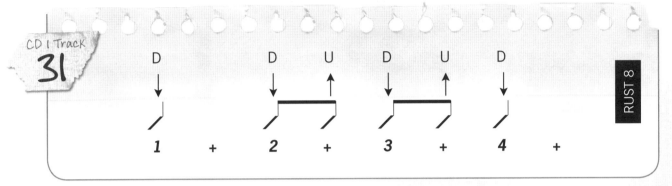

CD I Track **31**

RUST 8

Watching your hand

'Round about now, many people start to get worried about watching their strumming hand. When they do the fretting hand starts to go wrong and they get freaked out... when you are learning something new or checking for mistakes it is fine to watch your strumming hand, but try not to let that become the main thing you look at. You should try and develop a feel for it; let your strumming hand develop its own 'eyes' and find its way. This will happen a lot faster than you might expect, but you must have the confidence to let it go. Sometimes you will make mistakes, and that is OK, as long as you learn from them.

In conclusion: it's OK to watch you hand if you have to while you learn, but don't do it all the time!

Try your own

Feel free to make up your own patterns too, but only if you are 100% certain you understand the concepts and keep down-strums on each beat.

J.U.S.T.I.N. Training Exercises

Getting Started

Stage 1

Stage 2

Stage 3

Stage 4

Stage 5

Stage 6

Stage 7

Stage 8

Stage 9

Bonus

Chord Quality Recognition

At this stage we are still working out if chords are major or minor, but we're also going to compare them with a dominant 7 chord. I will be playing either D, Dm or D7 and you have to work out the type of chord played. This will take a little practice, but you're not scared of that, are you?

CD 1 Track
32

Sound Palette: major or minor or 7

CHORD		Attempt 1	Attempt 2	Attempt 3
	1.			
	2.			
	3.			
	4.			
	5.			

Single Sound Recognition

Now you should be working on hearing the chords fairly quickly too. Don't allow yourself to worry about it too much, just get in there and listen closely! Remember, we have also added in some of the 7th chords. Pause the track after the chord and try and get it right away. Make sure that you are listening out for whether the chord is major or minor or 7th, so you are not just guessing. If you have trouble telling two similar chords apart (like G and G7 or A and Am) try playing the one note that is different between the two chords for a while and then see if you can hear that note in the other chord. Playing the one note along with the recording should help your ear tell which is right!

CD 1 Track **33**

Chord Palette: E, A, D, Em, Am, Dm, G, C, G7, C7, B7, Fmaj7

CHORD		Attempt 1	Attempt 2	Attempt 3
	1.			
	2.			
	3.			
	4.			
	5.			

Chord Progression Recognition

As before, we're still working out our chord progressions, still with just one chord per bar, four strums on each. Please remember to pause after the chord so you can work it out. I still do that when I struggle with the changes, especially when they get fast. The more you work on this, the faster and easier it gets. It just takes practice. It gets fun too, even if right now it feels like hard work. Stick with it!

CD 1 Track **34**

Chord Palette: E, A, D, Em, Am, Dm, G, C, G7, C7, B7, Fmaj7

BAR		1.	2.	3.	4.
EXERCISE	1.				
	2.				
	3.				

If you need the answers, they're on page 93

Getting Started · Stage 1 · Stage 2 · Stage 3 · Stage 4 · Stage 5 · Stage 6 · Stage 7 · Stage 8 · Stage 9 · Bonus

89

Getting Started

Stage 1

Stage 2

Stage 3

Stage 4

Stage 5

Stage 6

Stage 7

Stage 8

Stage 9

Bonus

At Stage 4 we stick with a 30-minute workout.

Again, if you are finding this too much, then break it into two 15-minute practice sessions.

Things to remember

We're up to a half hour practice session now. If you can manage this every day you will see yourself progress very quickly and that can be really inspiring! But if that is simply too much then break it in half and alternate which things you do each day.

It's important that you practice things the right way so if you are even slightly uncertain about how to practice something then go back and revise the lesson or look back at the previous 'things to remember' tips and make sure you are doing it right. This will help you make the most of your practice time.

Chord sequences to try

This first sequence is one of the most common chord sequences of all time and there are a gazillion songs that use it… for a very clever example, search for 'The Axis Of Awesome: Four Chord Song' online and check out the very funny video where they combine over 50 tunes in a very funny sketch.

‖: C	G	Am	Fmaj⁷ :‖	‖: E	E	E	E	
					A	A	E	E
‖: C	G⁷	C	Fmaj⁷ :‖	B⁷	A	E	B⁷ :‖

‖: Am	G	B⁷	E :‖

‖: Am	G	C	C⁷	
Fmaj⁷	G	G⁷	C :‖

Stage 4 Practice chart (30 minutes)

Start date: _____

Work	Details	Time	M	T	W	T	F	S	S
Finger Workout		00:05:00							
Chord Practice	G7	00:01:00							
	C7	00:01:00							
	B7	00:01:00							
	Fmaj7	00:01:00							
	Pick a chord that needs work!	00:01:00							
One-Minute Changes (write in how many changes you did each day)	C to G7	00:01:00							
	C7 to Fmaj7	00:01:00							
	E to B7	00:01:00							
	? to ?	00:01:00							
	? to ?	00:01:00							
Rhythm Guitar	RUST 4	00:02:00							
	RUST 8	00:02:00							
Songs/Chord Sequences (write in details each day)		00:05:00							
J.U.S.T.I.N. Training	Chord Quality Recognition	00:02:00							
	Single Sound Recognition	00:02:00							
	Chord Progression Recognition	00:02:00							

Getting Started
Stage 1
Stage 2
Stage 3
Stage 4
Stage 5
Stage 6
Stage 7
Stage 8
Stage 9
Bonus

Stage 5

Getting Started

Stage 1

Stage 2

Stage 3

Stage 4

Stage 5

Stage 6

Stage 7

Stage 8

Stage 9

Bonus

 ## Introduction

Halfway through the course now! In this stage we've got some more dominant 7th chords and we're going to be looking at triplets and swinging rhythm. These will help you play some really cool blues songs!

We're also going to be looking at sharps and flats—what they are and how they work—in the Note Circle. This is an important piece of rudimentary musical knowledge.

We're also going to be learning how to change chords 'in the air' and look at a system to help you decide which chords you should be working on for your One-Minute Changes.

It's important now to make sure you fill in your practice routine to help keep you motivated. You are right in the thick of it now; many of the basic skills should be developing but you have a few key areas yet to work on that will really make the difference in your playing (mainly rhythmic things). So stay strong, practise as much as you can and enjoy the ride!

Getting Started
Stage 1
Stage 2
Stage 3
Stage 4
Stage 5
Stage 6
Stage 7
Stage 8
Stage 9
Bonus

BC-157

Here is a list of 10 songs—all included in the Justinguitar.com Beginner's Songbook—which you'll be able to play using the chords we'll have covered by the end of this stage:

Before You Accuse Me (Take A Look At Yourself) (Eric Clapton)

Folsom Prison Blues (Johnny Cash)

Sweet Little Angel (B. B. King)

Crossroads (Robert Johnson)

Evil (Is Going On) (Howlin' Wolf)

Mary Had A Little Lamb (Stevie Ray Vaughan)

Going Down Slow (Jimmy Witherspoon)

I Saw Her Standing There (The Beatles)

Mrs Robinson (Simon & Garfunkel)

That'll Be The Day (Buddy Holly)

J.U.S.T.I.N. TEST ANSWERS FOR STAGE 4

THE ANSWERS! NO PEEKING...

CQR: 1) D 2) D7 3) D 4) Dm 5) D7
SSR: 1) A 2) Em 3) G7 4) B7 5) C

CPR:

EXERCISE	BAR 1.	2.	3.	4.
1.	G	Am	C	Fmaj7
2.	C	G7	C	D
3.	G	B7	Em	C

93

Getting Started

Stage 1

Stage 2

Stage 3

Stage 4

Stage 5

Stage 6

Stage 7

Stage 8

Stage 9

Bonus

 Introduction

Next up we are looking at another three dominant 7th chords. With a total now of six 7th chords, you will be able to play a 12-bar blues in the keys of G, E, A and D!

 A7

This is a pretty straightforward chord: it only needs two fingers! Use whatever fingers you want—it doesn't really matter—it depends upon which

chords you are coming from and going to. This is the way that you should check it out first.

CD 1 Track
35

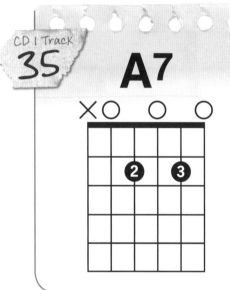
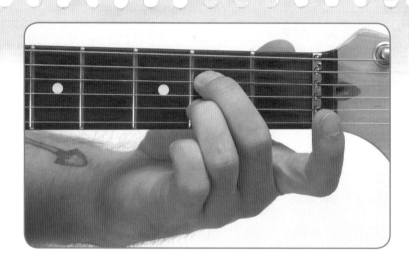

A7

X O   O   O

② ③

 D7

I think of this as looking a bit like a backwards D—see what I mean? This is an easy chord to play. The only common problem you might have is that your 2nd finger might fall too flat, which will make it mute the second string. Just make sure you are

using the tip of your finger to fret the note and it'll be fine.

Remember not to hit the fifth and sixth strings. Adding the fifth string won't matter too much but the sixth string will make this chord sound awful!

CD 1 Track
36

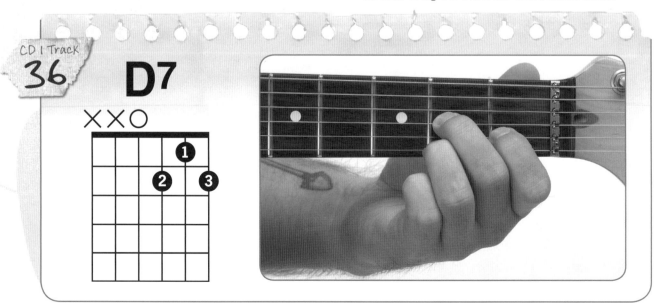

D7

X X O

①

② ③

Getting Started

Stage 1

Stage 2

Stage 3

Stage 4

Stage 5

Stage 6

Stage 7

Stage 8

Stage 9

Bonus

E7

This chord is the same as a regular E chord, but without using your 3rd finger. Easy! It can be a little tricky to get the fourth string ringing out clearly, and as that's the only note that is different from regular E, it's very important that it sounds. You will probably get this by making sure you use the very tips of your 1st and 2nd fingers.

CD 1 Track **37**

E7

In the photo above I moved my 3rd and 4th fingers out of the way so you can see the fingering clearly. It'll actually look more like the photo on the right when you're playing.

This chord can also be played by playing a regular E chord, and then adding your little finger at the 3rd fret, second string:

CD 1 Track **38**

E7

Getting Started

Stage 1

Stage 2

Stage 3

Stage 4

Stage 5

Stage 6

Stage 7

Stage 8

Stage 9

Bonus

Impress your mates with enharmonic equivalents!

At this point we're going to start learning just a tiny bit of music theory. A little theory goes a long way, and you will find your playing improves a lot with a little understanding of what you're doing. It's not too hard to grasp the basic principles, and you will use the information that we learn in this lesson forever!

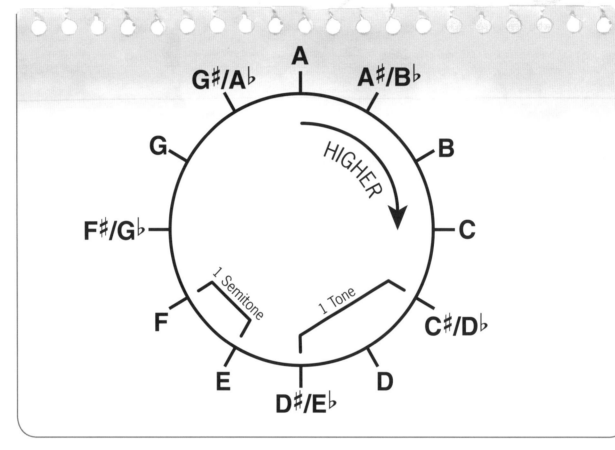

Here you can see here the 'Note Circle' which shows all 12 notes that we use in western music. Each step around the circle is the same as moving one fret, and this is called a semitone. Two steps around the circle is called a tone.

If you look at the 'white' notes (notes with no ♯ or ♭, like the white keys on a piano) you can see that they are all a tone apart, except for B and C and E and F, which are only a semitone apart. Did you ever notice that some white piano keys don't have a black key between them?

A sharp (♯) raises the pitch of a note by one semitone (one fret). An easy way to remember this is: if you sat on something sharp, you would jump up!

A flat (♭) lowers the pitch of a note by one semitone (one fret). The easy way to remember this one is that if your tyre is flat, it goes down.

One term that I really liked when I was learning this stuff in high school was the term 'enharmonic equivalent' which means two notes that sound the same but have different names, like A♯ and B♭. These two notes sound exactly the same (in our western 'equally tempered' music system).

You should get into counting your semitones, if you have a friend to help you, ask them to name any two notes and see if you can work out how many semitones there are between them. To start with you will probably have to look at the chart above, but try and get it into your memory as quickly as you can.

Remember that everything you learn should be memorized, not left on a page!

Air Changes

Change is in the air...

Up to now, you have probably been putting your fingers down one at a time when you play a chord, which is fine—it works—but there is another way, too. This is a more advanced technique which I have seen help a number of beginner guitarists. You will probably find it quite difficult to start off with, but once you get it, it will speed up your chord changes a lot.

The concept is pretty simple... all you do is form the finger positions for a chord in the air before you put any of your fingers down, and then put them down all at once. It is harder than it sounds (as you are sure to find out), but because all the fingers go down at the same time it can really give you a leap in your chord change speed.

You MUST START SLOWLY when you are learning this exercise or you might end up undoing some of your hard work in getting your chords sounding nice, as you will find that your fingers go down onto the wrong strings. Just do it slowly and try and get it right. Only when you have it right should you think about speeding up!

If you find yourself struggling you might find that it helps to put your fingers down in the reverse order from what you are used to.

Another tip is to try lifting and replacing the same chord, just so you get used to what the shape looks like in the air, which also gets you used to putting your fingers down all at once.

When you are playing songs you might like to keep using an anchor finger if there is one available. Most chord changes do not have one, which is why we have to learn 'air' changes. More often than not you have to form a whole new shape, and that is where this exercise really comes into its own.

It is a tricky one this, but well worth it, and you'll find it really does speed up your chord changes with a bit of practice. It might well take you a month to start feeling that you are making progress, but it's worth it. One of my students said he used to practise making the chords changes on his arm while on the train and that it made a huge difference, so that might be worth a try too. After all, it is really just about getting your fingers to be independent and to do different things at the same time! Good luck...

Getting Started

Stage 1

Stage 2

Stage 3

Stage 4

Stage 5

Stage 6

Stage 7

Stage 8

Stage 9

Bonus

97

One-Minute Changes

Getting Started

Stage 1

Stage 2

Stage 3

Stage 4

Stage 5

Stage 6

Stage 7

Stage 8

Stage 9

Bonus

Now we've got 'air changes' to work in, too.

At this stage, you need to pick five chords that you struggle to change between and just work on those. Everyone is different, and finds certain chords harder than others, so it is next to impossible for me to tell you which ones you should do!

You have now learnt 17 chords, and there are many possibilities for changes now—in fact, over 100 combinations— so how do you choose which changes to do?

Well, what I would recommend is that you look for chords that you find difficult that appear in a song that you are learning or want to learn. That way

you are working on chord changes that you will actually use.

So pick some chords, write them into your practice routine and off you go!

Usually I recommend a student can stop doing the One-Minute Changes once they reach 60 changes in a minute (playing each chord 30 times). The diagram below shows all the chords covered so far, so what I recommend is crossing them off when you have achieved the 60 changes per minute and then working on the ones you struggle with the most.

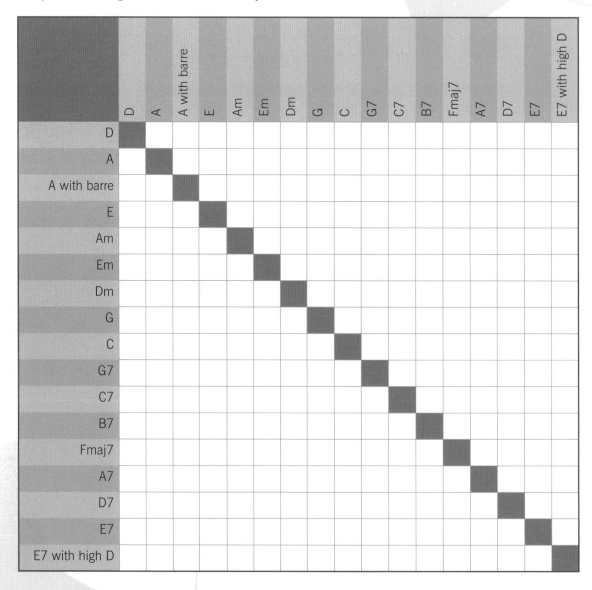

Remember: Practise what you can't do, not what you can!

Triplet Rhythms

Dividing into three

So far, all the rhythms we have looked at have four beats in the bar, with some of the beats divided into two. Now we are going to have a look at what happens when we divide a beat by three!

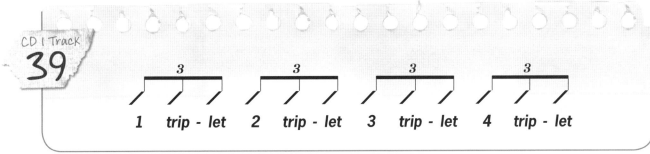

CD I Track
39

1 trip - let	**2** trip - let	**3** trip - let	**4** trip - let

Triplets

When a beat is divided into 3 you get a triplet. They have a different kind of feel compared to normal eighth notes (dividing a beat into two) and understanding them will help you find your blues groove.

They are usually written with the notes grouped together in threes and usually there is a '3' written under them too, so they should be quite easy to recognise.

Put your metronome on, and try and say the 'trip-let' count shown above along with the beat, making sure that the '1, 2, 3 and 4' stay right on the beat. This will get the feel of the triplet into your mind.

Getting Started

Stage 1

Stage 2

Stage 3

Stage 4

Stage 5

Stage 6

Stage 7

Stage 8

Stage 9

Bonus

Getting Started
Stage 1
Stage 2
Stage 3
Stage 4
Stage 5
Stage 6
Stage 7
Stage 8
Stage 9
Bonus

Swinging the rhythm

Now it is time to look at a shuffle rhythm, because it sounds cool when you are playing blues.

First of all, let's look at a bar with four beats in it, with each beat divided into three (triplets). As in the previous lesson, we count this with the number of the beat, then 'trip' and then 'let'.

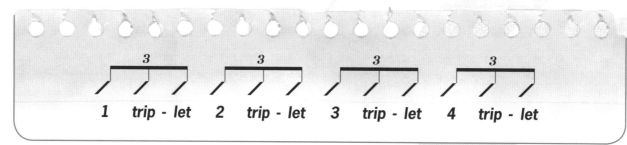

Then, we get rid of the middle note from each triplet, and we end up with a rhythm called a shuffle.

CD 1 Track **40**

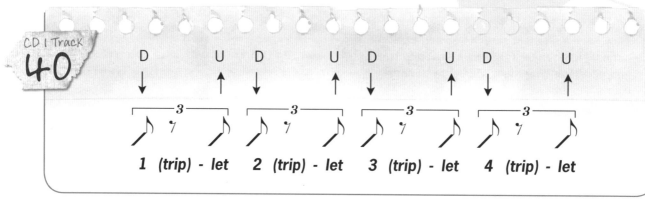

You can see that we still strum down on the beat, and we use an up-strum for the '-let'. So it is similar to the usual down-up pattern, but with the up-strum delayed slightly.

You can see there are four triplets in the bar. Counting as shown above while you play should help you know where you are. Say the 'trip', even though you are not playing it.

This shuffle-type of strumming has many variations and it not quite as 'tight' as I am showing you here. If you think of the first strum being right on the beat (which it should be) then the second strum (the up) can be anywhere in between where the 'and' would have been and the next beat, depending upon the groove you are playing.

For now you should work on getting the shuffle just as I have shown it in the above example, but be aware that in the future you might play around with this idea a bit. Listening to some songs with a shuffle rhythm will help you cop the groove.

Try to put this into practice, maybe playing a simple 12-Bar Blues using 7th chords and this shuffle strumming. You now know six dominant 7th chords, which means that you can play a 12-Bar progression in four different keys! (A, G, D and E) so you might like to try playing some of the blues songs listed on page 93, or look up some of your own; there are literally hundreds of songs that use the 12-Bar Blues progression!

12-bar blues sequences

Here are 12-Bar Blues chord progressions for blues in the keys of A, G, D and E, which you can play with the 7th chords that you now know. Play each chord for one bar for each time it is shown and try using the shuffle rhythm opposite.

Yes, the first chord is held for four bars, which does seem an awfully long time if you are playing a slow blues. I have made the blues in E and D into a 'quick change' blues which have a chord change in the second bar. Can you work out how to make the blues in A and G into 'quick changes'? I'm sure you can...

12-Bar Blues in A

A^7	A^7	A^7	A^7	
D^7	D^7	A^7	A^7	
E^7	D^7	A^7	E^7	

12-Bar Blues in G

G^7	G^7	G^7	G^7	
C^7	C^7	G^7	G^7	
D^7	C^7	G^7	D^7	

12-Bar Blues in E

E^7	A^7	E^7	E^7	
A^7	A^7	E^7	E^7	
B^7	A^7	E^7	B^7	

12-Bar Blues in D

D^7	G^7	D^7	D^7	
G^7	G^7	D^7	D^7	
A^7	G^7	D^7	A^7	

Remember, that you have a choice of ways of playing A7 and E7. Use whichever is most comfortable for you.

The most important thing is to be able to play all the way through without getting out of time or stopping, preferably with a metronome. Once you can do it at a slow tempo, gradually build the tempo up.

Any of you theory geeks that want to get into how a blues works might like to check out lesson BL-110 which explain the I, IV and V chords. In a more complex surrounding. But there is no need to go there unless you are really keen on learning the theory and already understand keys and chords in keys. If you don't understand those things you need to get Practical Music Theory.

Many people find counting uncomfortable and would rather do it by 'feel'. This is fine as long as you are 100% sure you are getting it 100% right. Otherwise, really work on your counting. Counting becomes more important later when the rhythms become complex (on a scale between 1 to 100 of rhythmic complexity, we're looking at about 3 right now, so there is a long way to go!). The good news is: it gets easier as you go on, too. Once you get the basics really solid then it becomes easier to add in new things.

There are many hundreds of blues songs that you can play if you know these sequences, For instance, 'Before You Accuse Me', 'Johnny B Goode', 'Carol'... actually, it's probably thousands. Many will have slight variations on the basic pattern shown above, but they usually work with these 'straight' sequences.

Have some fun with them and then have a go at some of those tunes...

Getting Started

Stage 1

Stage 2

Stage 3

Stage 4

Stage 5

Stage 6

Stage 7

Stage 8

Stage 9

Bonus

Getting Started

Stage 1

Stage 2

Stage 3

Stage 4

Stage 5

Stage 6

Stage 7

Stage 8

Stage 9

Bonus

Chord Quality Recognition

Now we step things up a bit... instead of our chords having the same root notes, the root note will change for each chord. However, all I want you to write down is the quality of the chord: major, minor or 7.

CD 1 Track
41

Sound Palette: major or minor or 7

CHORD		Attempt 1	Attempt 2	Attempt 3
	1.			
	2.			
	3.			
	4.			
	5.			
	6.			
	7.			
	8.			
	9.			
	10.			

Single Sound Recognition

The chord palette is growing now, so there are many choices! Take your time, pause the track and write down what chords I play. Go for it!

CD 1 Track 42

Chord Palette: E, A, D, Em, Am, Dm, G, C, G7, C7, B7, D7, E7, A7, Fmaj7

CHORD		Attempt 1	Attempt 2	Attempt 3
	1.			
	2.			
	3.			
	4.			
	5.			
	6.			
	7.			
	8.			
	9.			
	10.			

Chord Progression Recognition

We have a bit more going on now, because the number of times I strum a chord is going to change. Sometimes I will strum a chord four times, sometimes only twice. You can do it; just concentrate. You might find that it is a good idea to listen through the whole progression first so that you know when to pause and how often I am changing chords—just a little hint—sometimes chords will appear more than once, and you'll hear that by listening through the whole track.

CD 1 Track 43

Chord Palette: E, A, D, Em, Am, Dm, G, C, G7, C7, B7, D7, E7, A7, Fmaj7

BAR		1.	2.	3.	4.
EXERCISE	1.				
	2.				
	3.				

Answers for all this can be found on page 107!

Stage 5 Practice Schedule

Getting Started

Stage 1

Stage 2

Stage 3

Stage 4

Stage 5

Stage 6

Stage 7

Stage 8

Stage 9

Bonus

 ## 30 minutes

This is a 30-minute schedule; your fingers should be able to take a half-hour session by now without getting too sore, so it's just a question of whether you can find enough time to do it all. As usual, if you can't find the time, break the routine into two sessions and do 15 minutes each day. Just make sure you work on all the routine topics and not just the things you enjoy!

Things to explore

The blues is a wonderful vehicle for beginner guitar players… the chords are basically the same for many different songs!

If you have not listened much to the blues before then now might be a great time to get listening. Artists like B.B. King, Eric Clapton and Stevie Ray Vaughan are some amazing guitar players you might like to check out first. The older blues artists like Robert Johnson, Muddy Waters and Hubert

Sumlin (who played with Howlin' Wolf) are equally brilliant musicians, but their records are much more raw and many people find it hard work if they have not listened to much blues before.

Many of the great early rock and roll guitar players such as Chuck Berry, T-Bone Walker and even Elvis used a simple 12-Bar blues form, and it is still commonly used today.

Chord sequences to try

‖: A7	A7	A7	A7		‖: G7	G7	G7	G7
D7	D7	A7	A7		C7	C7	G7	G7
E7	D7	A7	E7 :‖		D7	C7	G7	D7 :‖

‖: E7	A7	E7	E7		‖: D7	G7	D7	D7
A7	A7	E7	E7		G7	G7	D7	D7
B7	A7	E7	B7 :‖		A7	G7	D7	A7 :‖

Some blues albums I particularly recommend are:

Live At The Regal – B.B. King (1965)
Couldn't Stand The Weather – Stevie Ray Vaughan & Double Trouble (1984)
Born Under a Bad Sign – Albert King (1967)
Live At The 1972 Monterey Jazz Festival – Jimmy Witherspoon & Robben Ford (1972)
Chess Box Set – Howlin' Wolf
King Of The Delta Blues – Robert Johnson (1961)
Bluesbreakers With Eric Clapton – John Mayall's Bluesbreakers (1966)
The Best Of – Chuck Berry

Stage 5 Practice chart (30 minutes)

Start date: _____

Work	Details	Time	M	T	W	T	F	S	S
Finger Workout		00:05:00							
Chord Practice	A7	00:01:00							
	D7	00:01:00							
	E7	00:01:00							
	Pick a chord that needs work!	00:01:00							
	Pick a chord that needs work!	00:01:00							
One-Minute Changes (write in how many changes you did each day)	? to ?	00:01:00							
	? to ?	00:01:00							
	? to ?	00:01:00							
	? to ?	00:01:00							
	? to ?	00:01:00							
Rhythm Guitar	RUST 8	00:02:00							
	Shuffle Rhythm	00:02:00							
Songs/Chord Sequences (write in details each day)		00:05:00							
J.U.S.T.I.N. Training	Chord Quality Recognition	00:02:00							
	Single Sound Recognition	00:02:00							
	Chord Progression Recognition	00:02:00							

Getting Started
Stage 1
Stage 2
Stage 3
Stage 4
Stage 5
Stage 6
Stage 7
Stage 8
Stage 9
Bonus

Stage 6

Getting Started

Stage 1

Stage 2

Stage 3

Stage 4

Stage 5

Stage 6

Stage 7

Stage 8

Stage 9

Bonus

 ## Don't be afraid... it's time to face the F Chord.

When I was learning I used to play lots of songs, but avoided any that had an F chord! It was too hard to play and I thought I'd just be able to get by without it. But I got there in the end, and so will you.

We're also going to be looking at the most commonly-used strumming pattern of all time! I refer to it often as 'old faithful' as it seems to have been used on so many songs. It's very important that you spend a lot of time with this one and make it feel really natural and instinctive.

We're also going to start doing some single note picking in preparation for playing some scales, and developing your pick accuracy!

Any of you using the Beginner's Songbook will have noticed capo positions in there and we're going to be looking more at capo use and how they work to move songs to new keys. It's good fun.

And if that wasn't enough we're also going to have a quick look at the basic set-up of guitars, so even if you are not actually going to try stuff like that yourself, you will understand what a a shop might tell you if you take them your guitar for repair or a set-up!

BC-167

Here is a list of 10 songs—all included in the Justinguitar.com Beginner's Songbook—which you'll be able to play using the chords you'll know by the end of this stage:

Please Forgive Me (David Gray)

All Along The Watchtower (Bob Dylan)

Hurt (Johnny Cash)

No Woman, No Cry (Bob Marley & The Wailers)

Can't Help Falling In Love (Elvis Presley)

Pink Bullets (The Shins)

The Thrill Is Gone (B.B. King)

Mr. Jones (Counting Crows)

Like A Rolling Stone (Bob Dylan)

House Of The Rising Sun (Traditional)

J.U.S.T.I.N. TEST ANSWERS FOR STAGE 5

THE ANSWERS! NO PEEKING...

COR: 1) E (maj) 2) Dm 3) C (maj) 4) G7
5) Am 6) C7 7) Am 8) G (maj) 9) A (maj)
10) D7

SSR: 1) Am 2) E7 3) Fmaj7 4) G7 5) Dm
6) G7 7) C7 8) Em 9) A 10) C

CPR:

EXERCISE	BAR: 1.	2.	3.	4.
1.	E G	E G	A C	A C
2.	E7	B7	E7	A7
3.	E	C D	E	G A

107

The Dreaded F Chord

Getting Started

Stage 1

Stage 2

Stage 3

Stage 4

Stage 5

Stage 6

Stage 7

Stage 8

Stage 9

Bonus

Everyone has to face this sometime... don't be scared. It won't hurt... much...

Being able to play F is a really important step and one that might take a month or more of frustration. I found it really hard when I first learnt it—really hard. But I often see students that try it during a lesson and can play it perfectly straight away, so try it and see how you go. This chord leads later to playing barre chords (which is the point at which you will ascend from being a beginner to an intermediate player!).

Try not to let yourself get discouraged if you find it hard. Try and think back to how hard it was to play your first chords and make them sound good. This one is no different really; once you get it you'll wonder why you ever had a problem with it at all!

If you have an electric and an acoustic guitar I would recommend learning this chord on your electric, which you'll probably find a lot easier. Get the technique good and you hand comfortable with the grip, and then move to acoustic; you're going to have to press a lot harder and have more finger strength, but your technique will be solid!

There are a few ways of playing this one. I'm going to try and introduce you to the hardest one first and see how you get on. Then we'll make it a little easier. When we learned the A chord with a barre, we held down more than one note at once with our first finger. For the F barre chord, you need to hold down all the strings at the first fret, with your other fingers in the positions shown:

CD 1 Track
44

F

If you're really struggling to get the barre, there are a couple of things you can try.

The best way to barre with your first finger is to turn it slightly on its side. So, start with it flat on the first fret and then roll it slightly back towards the nut so that it sits roughly halfway between the flat and the side of your finger.

If you have very old or very thick strings, then changing to nice new thin strings (9s on electric, 10s on acoustic) will almost certainly help because thin strings are easier to press down.

Make sure your 'action' is not too high, meaning that the strings are too far away from the fingerboard. This is usually adjusted in a guitar shop as part of a set-up. You'll have to pay for it, but a good set-up can make even a cheap guitar nice to play, and is usually worth the money.

Barre chords are easier when they are played further up the neck, so playing this shape at the 5th fret (which would make it an A chord actually) might be easier and allow you to build up the strength in your hand enough to go back to F. If not then try one of the variations opposite.

The first F chord below sounds more full than the lower one but its lowest note is a C note, so some people find it sounds strange. I don't; I like the sound of it better and in fact, I found it easier to play than the 'mini' variation shown at the bottom. For that chord, your 3rd finger should mute the fifth string; later, you might like to mute the thickest string with your thumb (but don't worry about that just yet, unless it comes really easy!).

CD 1 Track
45

F

CD 1 Track
46

F

 ## Common problems with playing F:

"My B string buzzes"

Oh, if I had a dollar for every time I heard that! It's just because your barre is not strong enough yet. You should make sure that the barre is rolled a little onto its side. Most likely it's just going to take some time to get your muscles strong enough to hold your finger in place.

"I can play it, but it's so slow to get to it, I'll never be able to use it in a song"

Think back to your slow changes when you

started. Most people need to spend quite a lot of time doing One-Minute changes with the F to even start to get the changes smooth. It's going to take you some time, but once you are over this hurdle the rest is plain sailing.

"Perhaps I need to buy one of those hand-strengthening machines"

No you don't, just practise more! Those things are a waste of time. Do your workout on the guitar!

Getting Started

Stage 1

Stage 2

Stage 3

Stage 4

Stage 5

Stage 6

Stage 7

Stage 8

Stage 9

Bonus

Getting Started

Stage 1

Stage 2

Stage 3

Stage 4

Stage 5

Stage 6

Stage 7

Stage 8

Stage 9

Bonus

 ## We've got a whole heap of chords by this stage...

...and so you have some work to do! Now that we have introduced the F chord, you have to work on every chord that we've looked at so far and its change to F... or do you?

What you will find as you progress is that some chords sound good combined with other chords, and some sound a bit odd. Up to this point we've been looking at changing between all the chords to get your fingers working well, but now I want you to start to focus on chord changes that you will actually use.

F to C **3rd finger stays in position as an anchor**

F to E **Slide the barre off and use fingers 2/3/4 to play the E Chord!***

F to Dm **All change**

F to Am **All change**

F to G **All change**

* Playing the E chord with fingers 2, 3 and 4 is not normally recommended, but is very useful sometimes. It's for you to work out when, because it really depends on the situation.

The examples I have given you here are chords which are very often heard in songs with F so they will all need work, but from now on I want you to think about the chord changes you actually need to use for the songs you want to play. So, if you come across a chord change that you find difficult in a song, add it into your One-Minute Changes! Even if that part of your schedule is full, add it in there and do that extra minute in your practice session. You know better than anyone what chords you need to work on the most, because you know what songs you play and what you want to play!

So after working on the examples above, think carefully about the ones you will work on next!

Getting Started

Stage 1

Stage 2

Stage 3

Stage 4

Stage 5

Stage 6

Stage 7

Stage 8

Stage 9

Bonus

A capo is a very useful little device that enables you to use the same chord shapes to play songs in different keys.

It is wise for singers to move a song into a key that suits their voice. A capo is also used to simplify some songs that would otherwise require barre chords. It doesn't work with all songs (for some, you simply have to learn barre chords) but for many tunes, a capo is a great option.

They are not just for beginners, either. Some players seem to think they are a beginner's tool, but they become more and more interesting the longer you play, because they expand the possibilities of the guitar, which is great fun. So don't be put off by any capo snobs, they don't know what they are talking about!

It is important that you put the capo just behind the fret (the same as you should be doing with your fingers too!) or you will get lots of buzzing sounds. Have a look at the picture here; note that the capo is right behind the fretwire, not actually on it.

Each of the chords you play in open position can be played using a capo, but if you do that, the name of the chord changes; it goes up one semitone for every fret the capo is moved up. So an open G chord with a capo on the 1st fret will become a G# chord. With the capo on the 2nd fret it will become an A chord, and so on. Try it now and hear for yourself:

Play an open A chord. Then put the capo on fret 2, and play a G chord. They sound more or less the same!

Because of this, capos can be used in some circumstances to replace barre chords. Let's say the chords in the song you want to play have the chords Bm, E and A in it, but you don't know how to play Bm. However, you can get a Bm by playing an A minor with the capo on the 2nd fret! Check the other chords and you'll find you can get an E chord by playing a D, and an A chord by playing G. See the bonus section at the back of the book for more on this.

The above trick doesn't always work, but it very often does, and can mean that you can play some songs that you previously thought you couldn't. It's this concept that I used for many of the songs in the songbook so you could play along with the original recordings using basic chords.

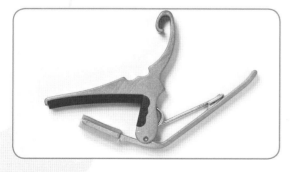

Get the capo right behind the fret.

There seems to be a lot of debate about the correct pronunciation of the word. I say it cap-o, others say Kay-po, it seems to be a English vs U.S. thing. But who cares? Not me!

Getting Started

Stage 1

Stage 2

Stage 3

Stage 4

Stage 5

Stage 6

Stage 7

Stage 8

Stage 9

Bonus

Basic guitar adjustments

For most problems you might have with your instrument it is probably best to take your guitar to a guitar shop, but I think it's a good idea to understand the basics of guitar set-up a bit anyhow, so that you understand what they're telling you in the shop. Those good with their hands can have a go if they feel confident!

Action

The 'action' is the measurement of how far the strings are from the fingerboard. If the action is too low, the strings will buzz a lot when you play. If it's too high, then it will be very difficult to play anything.

If the action needs adjusting on an acoustic, you really need to take the guitar to a shop and have it set-up. On electric, you can try adjusting the bridge saddles (with an Allen key on a Stratocaster-type guitar, or a screwdriver for Gibson-type guitars). There is not too much that can go seriously wrong, but if you really make a pig's ear of it, you will just have to take it to the shop and get them to sort out your mess!

Tremolo systems

If you have a Stratocaster-type tremolo system, then I would recommend tightening the screws in the back of the guitar and or adding five springs, effectively locking the tremolo against the body of the guitar so it doesn't work. As a beginner you are unlikely to use it in a musical way anyway, and your guitar will stay in tune a lot better this way.

If you got yourself a guitar with a locking tremolo system then you'll have to take it to a shop, or be prepared for some major headaches.

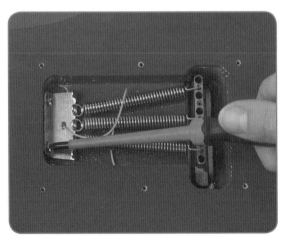

The nut

If the nut needs adjusting, I would say take it in for professional help, they will require filing which is impossible to undo! If the strings are clicking (pinging) in the nut then they might need some lubrication. Graphite is best: get a pencil and simply draw in the groove!

Strap pin fix

One very simple trick I can share with you is for fixing a loose strap button (the thing that the strap clips to) If it's loose, unscrew it, and then coat a matchstick in wood glue and ram it into the hole. Once the glue has dried just screw it back in place. The wood used in matches in not very dense so you should have no problem getting the screw back in. DON'T try this with acoustic guitars, only electrics! Of course, I can't be responsible if something goes wrong…

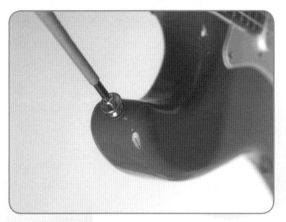

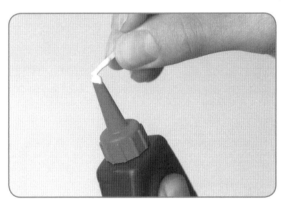

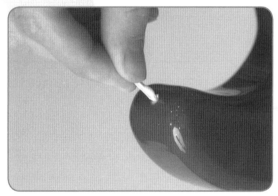

Two other tips

- **Don't leave your guitar right near a heat source: a radiator, a fireplace or in the hot sun. The wood could warp and totally ruin your instrument.**

- **Don't lean your guitar against the wall or a table; lay it down flat where it has no place to fall, or buy a stand. Leaning it against the edge of a table, against a wall or in a chair is just asking for trouble!**

Getting Started

Stage 1

Stage 2

Stage 3

Stage 4

Stage 5

Stage 6

Stage 7

Stage 8

Stage 9

Bonus

113

Getting Started

Stage 1

Stage 2

Stage 3

Stage 4

Stage 5

Stage 6

Stage 7

Stage 8

Stage 9

Bonus

Now we are going to introduce ties.

You don't wear these ties around your neck, you tie notes together with them! They have the effect of making strumming patterns sound more natural than those we have looked at up until now. EVERYONE struggles with these a little when they first have a go at them, but if you follow my advice you should be fine. The pattern we are going to learn is probably the most common strumming pattern of all time. It is really easy and sounds great.

Look back to the previous strumming pattern, shown again here, and then we are going to incorporate a tie.

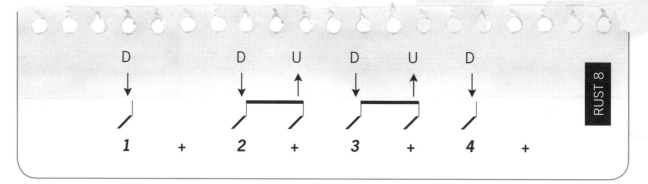

So, first of all, what is a tie? Well, a tie is a little curved line that goes between two notes and 'ties' those two notes together. For pattern number eight you will see that you have got the count of 'one, two and three and four'. Now, if you tie the middle two notes together, it means that you don't play the second of the two. So you would count '1, 2 and, and 4'; you don't strum on '3'; you let the chord ring on from the 'and' after '2'. Have a listen to this rhythm on the CD:

CD 1 Track
47

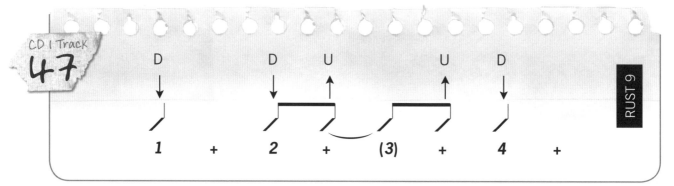

There is only one 'trick' to this, and that is the trick to all strumming patterns: KEEP YOUR HAND MOVING. Don't let it pause after the up-strum before the tie and then have to rush down to get the next up-strum. This is the most common mistake that people make. Keep that hand moving!

Once you can play it, you need to do it over and over again—drill it in so that it becomes natural to do it. This for many guitarists is THE strumming pattern, and I have met quite a few singer-songwriters that use this pattern in every song! That's not necessarily recommended, but you will use this pattern a whole lot once you get it comfortable.

This pattern comes up so often, I call it 'old faithful'. You can rely on it to work most of the time!

Picking Individual Strings

Because we will be looking at playing some scales soon, I want you to get used to picking out one string at a time.

This a very simple exercise to help get you started. It should be easy; the thing to work on is accuracy, not speed. There are better exercises to work on speed, which we will look at later, but for now just try and make sure that you only pluck one string at a time. If you've been using a thin gauge pick up to now, you might like to try a thicker one for this type of exercise.

This exercise just uses the open strings, so you can relax your fretting hand now (although you might like to mute the open strings by lightly resting that hand on the strings. ⊓ means pick down; ∨ means pick up. These are symbols derived from classical music, but you'll see them a lot in guitar transcriptions.

CD 1 Track
48

Exercise 1: One pick on each string, all down-picks

Exercise 2: One pick on each string, all up-picks

Exercise 3: Two picks on each string, down then up

Exercise 4: Four picks on each string, down/up/down/up

It's likely that you will sometimes pick the wrong strings when you start out. That's normal. Surprise, surprise: it will take practice to get right. I find it best to anchor my picking hand little finger on the scratch plate to help my pick find the right strings.

Don't be worried if your little finger is touching the thinnest string when you are playing the thickest one. This is normal, even desirable!

This is really to get you warmed up for playing scales which are one of the best ways of increasing your pick accuracy, so just have a go and get warmed-up for the next stage, when we start looking at scales.

Getting Started
Stage 1
Stage 2
Stage 3
Stage 4
Stage 5
Stage 6
Stage 7
Stage 8
Stage 9
Bonus

Getting Started

Stage 1

Stage 2

Stage 3

Stage 4

Stage 5

Stage 6

Stage 7

Stage 8

Stage 9

Bonus

Chord Quality Recognition

Here we're continuing on from the last stage, just working on the same three qualities. Take it slow, focus on the quality of the chord (not how well I play it, silly! The type of chord it is…) Try and get a feeling for each of the chords; eventually you want to know the chord by feeling, not analysis!

CD 1 Track
49

Sound Palette: major, minor or 7

		Attempt 1	Attempt 2	Attempt 3
CHORD	1.			
	2.			
	3.			
	4.			
	5.			
	6.			
	7.			
	8.			
	9.			
	10.			

justinguitar.com

Getting Started

Stage 1

Stage 2

Stage 3

Stage 4

Stage 5

Stage 6

Stage 7

Stage 8

Stage 9

Bonus

Single Sound Recognition

The chord palette is growing now, so there are many choices! Take your time, pause the track, and write down what chords I play. Before you just guess, really try and listen to the quality of the chord. Try and hear how many thick strings are being played, because that can give you a hint to the chord, and you should be looking for all the clues that you can find.

I play the chords a little faster now, so you have to work on your pause technique. It also means that you will hear the chord for a slightly shorter time now as well, which makes you work a little harder.

CD 1 Track
50

Chord Palette: E, A, D, Em, Am, Dm, G, C, G7, C7, B7, D7, E7, A7, Fmaj7

		Attempt 1	Attempt 2	Attempt 3
CHORD	1.			
	2.			
	3.			
	4.			
	5.			
	6.			
	7.			
	8.			
	9.			
	10.			

Chord Progression Recognition

As in the last stage, I will be playing the chords for either two or four strums in each bar. Try and hear when a sequence goes back to a chord that has been played before; it can speed things up quite a lot when you get that skill down.

Remember that there are four strums per bar, so writing down how many times a chord is strummed in each bar is a good idea.

CD 1 Track
51

Chord Palette: E, A, D, Em, Am, Dm, G, C, G7, C7, B7, D7, E7, A7, Fmaj7

BAR		1.	2.	3.	4.
EXERCISE	1.				
	2.				
	3.				

Only look at the answers if you really have to! (Page 121)

Stage 6 Practice Schedule

Getting Started

Stage 1

Stage 2

Stage 3

Stage 4

Stage 5

Stage 6

Stage 7

Stage 8

Stage 9

Bonus

Off to work!

Now we have added another exercise and split up the five minutes of technical work. Make sure you are using your timer, and make full use of the two minutes that you are working on on the finger workout. The timer will help keep you focused!

Things to remember

F is going to be hard. It's going to take some work. But don't be discouraged; pretty much everyone struggles with it, which is why it has such a bad reputation! But it's nice once you get to know it!

Being able to play F cleanly is partly to do with muscle strength, which will take time and practice to develop. Yes, having a good technique will help a whole lot, but it's also just going to take some time to get used to, and changing chords to and from it will also take time to get right.

Chord sequences to try

| 𝄆 F | C | Am | Dm 𝄇 | | 𝄆 C | F | C | G |
| | | | | | | C | Am | F | G 𝄇 |

| 𝄆 C | G⁷ | C | Fmaj⁷ 𝄇 |

| | | | | | 𝄆 F | C | F | G |
| 𝄆 Am | F | G | E⁷ 𝄇 | | Am | C | Dm | E 𝄇 |

Stage 6 Practice chart (30 minutes)

Start date: _____

Work	Details	Time	M	T	W	T	F	S	S
Finger Workout		00:02:00							
Basic Picking Exercise		00:02:00							
Chord Practice*	F (version 1)	00:02:00							
	F (version 2)	00:02:00							
	F (version 3)	00:02:00							
One-Minute Changes (write in how many changes you did each day)	F to C	00:01:00							
	F to E	00:01:00							
	F to D	00:01:00							
	F to Am	00:01:00							
	F to G	00:01:00							
Rhythm Guitar	RUST 9	00:04:00							
Songs/Chord Sequences (write in details each day)		00:05:00							
J.U.S.T.I.N. Training	Chord Quality Recognition	00:02:00							
	Single Sound Recognition	00:02:00							
	Chord Progression Recognition	00:02:00							

* If you have got the hang of the full barre chord F, put in six minutes on that;
   don't worry about the easier versions.

Getting Started

Stage 1

Stage 2

Stage 3

Stage 4

Stage 5

Stage 6

Stage 7

Stage 8

Stage 9

Bonus

Stage 7

Getting Started

Stage 1

Stage 2

Stage 3

Stage 4

Stage 5

Stage 6

Stage 7

Stage 8

Stage 9

Bonus

 ## Introduction

Welcome to Stage 7. We've got a whole lot of cool stuff to do in this stage. Most people find they spend a little longer on this stage than the previous sections to get everything under their fingers. We're going to start taking a look at Power Chords, Suspended chords, our first scale (don't worry, it's easy and you'll really enjoy using it later in the course!), a little general knowledge learning the notes on the neck in open position, and a really cool strumming pattern which makes simple open chords sound awesome!

I want to mention to you that I'm going to include some notation (dots) as well as TAB in the examples of scales and stuff. You don't have to read it; I have included it in case people on other instruments want to play them with you, or for teachers that might be helping you with the book that read traditional notation.

So, there's lots to be getting on with here. Just take it easy; make sure you feel comfortable playing power chords because we're going to develop them more in the next stage, and it will be best if you have sixth-string root chords sounding good before moving on.

Remember to try and put these new chords into use too, especially the sus chords. You really have to practise using them to work them into your playing. They sound really slick when you get them sounding effortless and natural—There are some song examples which use these chords in the Justinguitar.com Beginner's Songbook, or see more suggestions on the website!

Justinguitar.com

Getting Started

Stage 1

Stage 2

Stage 3

Stage 4

Stage 5

Stage 6

Stage 7

Stage 8

Stage 9

Bonus

BC-177

Here is a list of 10 songs—all included in the Justinguitar.com Beginner's Songbook—which you can play using the chords we'll have covered by the end of stage 7:

Summer Of '69 (Bryan Adams)

Wanted Dead Or Alive (Bon Jovi)

Lucky Man (The Verve)

California Dreamin' (The Mamas & The Papas)

Don't You (Forget About Me) (Simple Minds)

You Really Got Me (The Kinks)

Have A Nice Day (Stereophonics)

Love Is All Around (The Troggs)

Down Under (Men At Work)

Weather With You (Crowded House)

J.U.S.T.I.N. TEST ANSWERS FOR STAGE 6

THE ANSWERS! NO PEEKING...
CGR: 1) Am 2) A7 3) Em 4) E (maj)
5) G (maj) 6) Em 7) C7 8) Dm 9) B7
10) C (maj)
SSR: 1) C 2) G7 3) Fmaj7 4) Em 5) A7
6) Fmaj7 7) E 8) D 9) Am 10) C7

CPR:

BAR:	1.	2.	3.	4.
EXERCISE 1.	E	A	D	A
2.	G	C	G	D
3.	G	C	G	Am

Getting Started

Stage 1

Stage 2

Stage 3

Stage 4

Stage 5

Stage 6

Stage 7

Stage 8

Stage 9

Bonus

 It is important to learn the names of the notes found around the nut.

This will give you a better understanding of why you play chords a certain way, what the notes are in the chords, and also help your general musicianship, which will help in pretty much every aspect of your playing! Little things like this really make a bigger difference than it might seem at first, and I'm sure you will find this valuable if you take the time to study it.

The diagram on the right shows all the notes up to the fifth fret.

The notes we are most concerned with are the notes in the first three frets. These MUST be memorised now.

Start by learning the 'white' notes. Make sure you also work out the sharps and flats in between those notes. You will find this easy to do if you have learned your Note Circle (BC-152, page 96).

Notice that E and F, and B and C, are always next to each other (remember that they are only a semitone apart) and that all the others have a fret (and note) between them.

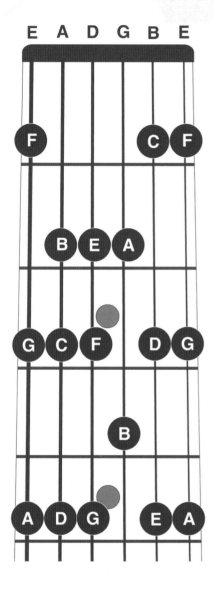

 Suggested Exercise

Play any open chord that you know and then work out what the notes are that you are playing. What I want you to get good at is working out the notes in the open position quickly and easily.

Once you can do this, you will find it relatively easy to work out notes all over the neck. You might have to count your way up the neck a little further, but it's really no harder!

Try working out the notes for every chord we have looked at so far in the course and write down what the notes are. You might even start to see similarities between how each chord is made up.

So here we go into rock guitar!

'Power' Chords are used in most styles of music but are particularly useful for rock guitar; they even sound cool on acoustic (check out Nirvana's *Unplugged* album for an awesome example). The basic idea is that you only have to learn one chord shape, and that one shape can move around the fingerboard to make other chords. It uses no open strings, and muting the unused open strings is a very important part of the technique.

Let's start by playing some power chords, and we'll do the theory later.

CD I Track
52

G5

Use your 1st, 3rd and 4th fingers as shown, and start by putting your 1st finger in the 3rd fret of the sixth string (the note G). Then put down your 3rd and 4th fingers. If this is a bit of stretch, don't worry, you will soon limber up! Try to keep them together, the 3rd finger kind of on top of the 4th as shown.

Some people like to play the two notes on 5th and 4th strings with a small barre with the 3rd finger. It's O.K. to do that, but I think using two fingers gives you a better finger position on the notes; you'll get a better sound that way, it makes it easier to change chords most of the time and easier to get all the thin strings muted. I strongly advise to learn it this way, and then if you still prefer to use the little barre you have the option of choosing whichever one works best in any situation!

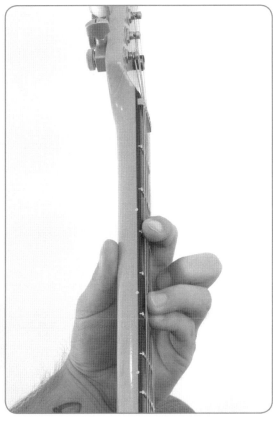

Try and keep your middle finger relaxed just hanging out where it feels good (shown in the top photo). Don't try and pull it down to the thin strings; sometimes I do that but only when trying to show the chords in lessons (as shown in the lower picture!)

Getting Started

Stage 1

Stage 2

Stage 3

Stage 4

Stage 5

Stage 6

Stage 7

Stage 8

Stage 9

Bonus

Getting Started

Stage 1

Stage 2

Stage 3

Stage 4

Stage 5

Stage 6

Stage 7

Stage 8

Stage 9

Bonus

 ## Muting the unused strings

Try to get your 1st finger to lay softly on strings 3, 2 and 1. You don't want those notes to sound; you just want to mute the strings. This is very important as it will sound really bad if you let them ring out.

You could just try to be careful, and only play the three strings of the chord, but that is really hard. It means that you will never be able to rock out and hit the strings with any energy, or run around on stage like a rock god…

With a super-low action you might have trouble muting the strings because they will require so little pressure to sound, but you must. It's the downside of having such a low action. You'll find barre chords easy, but it's going to take a light touch and lots of practice to get those notes muted properly.

Quite often, power chords are played with only down-strums, and often with a technique called palm muting, which might make it less vital to mute the unused strings. But it is REALLY important to mute them because many songs do use up- and down-strums with power chords ('Smells Like Teen Spirit' springs to mind). Also, if you don't mute them, and you play loud with distortion, the strings might ring out—even if you don't pick them—and which will make your chords sound messy. So make sure you get your string muting sorted now!

Root notes

Each chord has a 'Root Note', as shown in this chord diagram:

G5

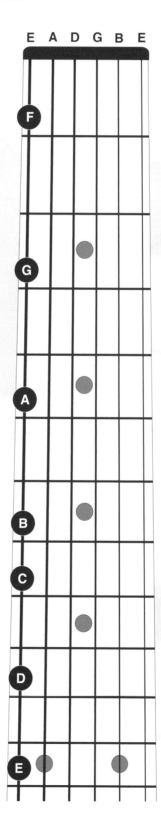

Once you know that, we can move the chord around. Have a look at the notes on the sixth (thickest) string, shown on the right. The example we just played was a G power chord (also called G5) because the root note under the 1st finger is the note G. If we move the shape up the neck, we can play other chords. For instance, if you move it up two frets you get the chord A, because that is the root note you'll find under your 1st finger.

It is a big concept that will help you advance on the guitar, so take the time to learn where all the notes are.

The Notes In Between

You should now know all the notes in between the 'white' notes from your study of the note circle (page 96). Eventually, you should try and remember ALL the notes on the thickest two strings. You will use these time and time again, so they really need to be in your memory, not 'left on the page'.

Playing power chords right up at the 'dusty' end (past the 8th fret) gets difficult, because the frets are so close together. In the next stage we'll learn how to play power chords with a fifth-string root too, which solves that problem. However, it's important not to rush ahead, so make sure you put your effort just into the sixth-string root chords for now.

This root note concept applies to many things on guitar. In fact, it applies to pretty much everything

that does not use open strings. All scales and chords that don't use open strings can just be moved up and down the neck. As long as you know which note is the root note, you will be able to find that chord or scale.

Getting Started

Stage 1

Stage 2

Stage 3

Stage 4

Stage 5

Stage 6

Stage 7

Stage 8

Stage 9

Bonus

Getting Started

Stage 1

Stage 2

Stage 3

Stage 4

Stage 5

Stage 6

Stage 7

Stage 8

Stage 9

Bonus

Suspended chords sound like their name.

They can be used as chord in their own right, or can be used to embellish a chord sequence. They are very commonly used, and once you learn them, you will start to hear them being used when you listen to music, because the sound is quite distinctive. They are pretty easy to play; the big task is to try and work them into your playing so that they just happen naturally without having to think about it too much.

Asus4

There are many ways to finger this chord. The fingering shown here is pretty standard, but would be the fingering you used if you're using this chord as part of a progression with A—if that chord is fingered the 'Old Skool' way, with the three fingers in a row—in which case you just add in your 4th finger to make the Asus4. You can leave the 3rd finger behind the 4th it if you like, it makes no difference.

If you have learned A the way I recommend you will still add your 4th finger but the 1st and 2nd

fingers will be swapped over, as shown in the lower photo and diagram.

You can also play it by sliding your 3rd finger forward from either A shape. If you were playing an A with a mini-barre (page 83) you would probably use your 3rd finger to play the 'suspended' note, but it doesn't matter which finger you use.

From an Am chord you would just add your 4th finger.

CD 1 Track

53

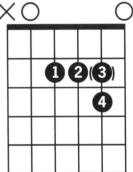

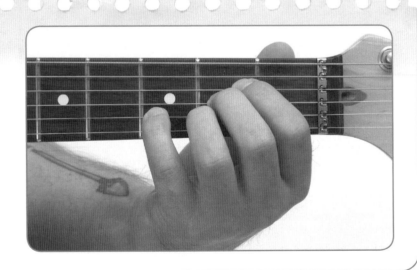

Old skool fingering shown above; My way shown here below:

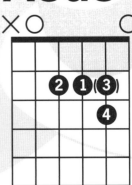

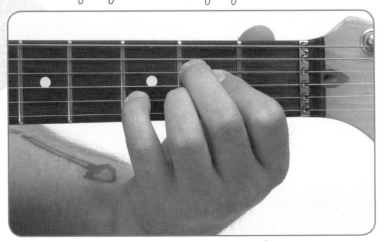

126

justinguitar.com

Getting Started

Stage 1

Stage 2

Stage 3

Stage 4

Stage 5

Stage 6

Stage 7

Stage 8

Stage 9

Bonus

Asus2

This again is the 'Old Skool' fingering. If you are doing this course and have learned the A chord with my recommended version then the fingering shown will be swapped around, as shown at the bottom of the page. From Am, you would just lift off your 1st finger and use fingers 2/3.

If it's 'old skool', why am I telling you about it? Well I'm glad you asked… The fingering that I show you for the A chord way back in the early

lessons is great when you're starting to learn your chord changes, but sometimes that fingering can get in the way. I find using sus chords with 'my' fingering can be pretty uncomfortable, so I guess that you might too. Realistically, you want to be able to play an A chord in three ways: the way that I taught you, the 'old' method and the mini-barre method. Each one has pros and cons in different circumstances, so learn all of them!

CD 1 Track
54

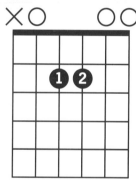

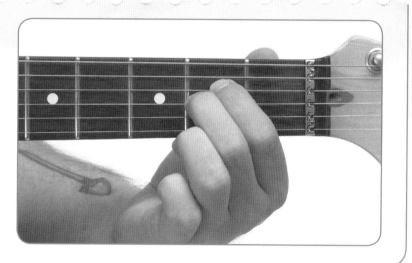

The 'old skool' way…

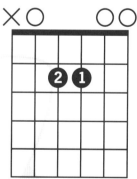

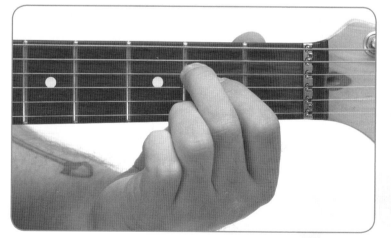

…My way!

Getting Started
Stage 1
Stage 2
Stage 3
Stage 4
Stage 5
Stage 6
Stage 7
Stage 8
Stage 9
Bonus

 ## Dsus4 and Dsus2

These two variations are usually used in conjunction with D or Dm. You'll hear them a lot; they are often used as an embellishment to regular chord progressions ('Wanted Dead or Alive' by Bon Jovi is an excellent example). They are pretty easy to play, easy to remember, they don't need any funny fingering changes, and sound cool.

 ## Dsus4

This is just like playing a regular D chord but with your little finger added under your 3rd finger. Pretty easy, really! Of course if you're coming from a Dm chord, the fingers will be different again; Just remember that as long as you have the right

dots pressed down that it is not important which fingers you use. In this case you will probably be using your 2nd, 3rd and 4th fingers to fret a Dsus4 chord coming from Dm.

CD 1 Track 55 **Dsus⁴**

 ## Dsus2

For this chord, start with a regular D, and then lift off your 2nd finger. Make sure that your 3rd finger is not touching the 1st string or it won't sound, and then it will not sound 'suspended'!

CD 1 Track 56 **Dsus²**

 **Esus4**

This is generally the fingering that you use for a Esus4, whether you have come from E (major) or Em. Note that there is not a proper open chord for Esus2. There is a way of playing it, but no one uses it very often, it's not very easy and sounds a little strange, so I have left it out.

CD 1 Track 57

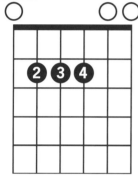

 A touch of theory

Chords are generally made up of three notes, called a root, 3rd and 5th: the first, third and fifth notes of a major scale. It's the 3rd that makes a chord major or minor. Perhaps you've noticed that only one note changes when we change a chord from major to minor? That's the 3rd.

'Suspended' basically means "take away the third and replace with…" so suspended chords are neither major or minor, and that is why they sound so cool, but also why they want to 'resolve' to a major or minor chord.

 How to practise sus chords

Sus chords can be used either as a cool-sounding chords in their own right or as 'ornamental' chords that you might use to embellish a simple chord progression. This second way is the most common way to use them so the best way to play them is with their 'parent' chords (both major and minor).

For example, you might play D – Dsus4 – D – Dsus2 over and over. Get used to embellishing the D chord with the suspended sounds. Then you might try Dm – Dsus2 – Dm – Dsus4 – Dm so that you get used to the sus sounds with the minors too. These are really cool chords to get down.

Do that with each set of chords and listen out for them in the 'real' world because you can copy ideas once you have heard them and got the sound stuck in your head.

Getting Started

Stage 1

Stage 2

Stage 3

Stage 4

Stage 5

Stage 6

Stage 7

Stage 8

Stage 9

Bonus

One-Minute Changes

Getting Started

Stage 1

Stage 2

Stage 3

Stage 4

Stage 5

Stage 6

Stage 7

Stage 8

Stage 9

Bonus

'Knowing' sus chords is not good enough...

...you must play them until they become instinctive, because you want to be able to add them so they come out naturally when you play. To make this happen you have to practise using them, which is why I have given you these changes here.

Also, at this stage you should probably still be working on changes from and to F, as they are the hardest changes! However, you should also spend some time looking at these new sus chords, too.

A – Asus4 – A – Asus2
D – Dsus4 – D – Dsus2
F to ?
F to ?
F to ?

This is worth learning even if you're not a country music fan.

This is a slightly more advanced rhythm guitar pattern. In this pattern we separate out the bass note of the chord and the actual strum. It is a really cool-sounding technique and it can make your rhythm playing sound a lot more interesting.

Try this, with a G chord—have a look at the tab and strumming pattern below. below.

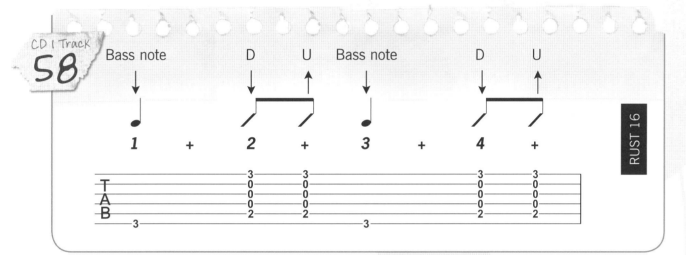

CD 1 Track 58

RUST 16

On beats 1 and 3, just pick the thickest string. That is the note G from our G chord: the bass note of the chord. Then, on beats 2 and 4, you strum down and then up.

Now it is really important to understand that every chord has a different bass note. We already did a little bit of work to learn what the notes are in the open position. So, if we are looking at the Am chord, you should be able to know that the bass

note for the Am chord is going to be the open fifth string, and so that is the note you'll play. If we went to an open C chord then you should know that the lowest C note that we are playing is the note at the 3rd fret of the fifth string. If we went to a D chord, you should know again that the lowest D note is, right up on the open fourth string. Have a go at this chord progression, as tabbed out here, to try these chords:

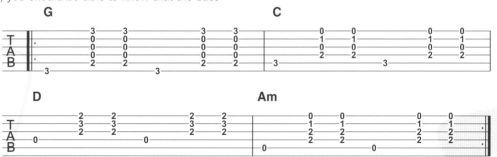

This is a really nice pattern to learn. Because you have to focus on individual notes, you are really concentrating on what you are playing. It gives you good pick control because you don't want to be sitting there just randomly thrashing away at the guitar all of the time. This teaches you to be quite accurate even within a strum, because strumming is generally kind of loose. When you start doing these individual picks you have to be both relaxed and accurate at the same time.

You can do all sorts of tricky stuff as you get better and more accurate with your picking hand. This is one pattern you can use on loads of different songs. Any songs that you like that you have learnt so far. Have a go at sticking the bass note in, making sure you know what the bass note is for every chord that you are playing and then just experiment!

Getting Started

Stage 1

Stage 2

Stage 3

Stage 4

Stage 5

Stage 6

Stage 7

Stage 8

Stage 9

Bonus

The Minor Pentatonic Scale

Getting Started

Stage 1

Stage 2

Stage 3

Stage 4

Stage 5

Stage 6

Stage 7

Stage 8

Stage 9

Bonus

 This is the most common scale in blues, pop and rock music.

It is easy to learn and is essential for learning to improvise in a blues style. 'Penta' means five and 'tonic' means note, so 'Minor Pentatonic Scale' really just means 'Minor Five-Note Scale'.

The reason we learn scales is that they are groups of notes that sound really good together that we can use to make up solos (as in lead guitar) and melodies. We'll get to that later on. They are also great for developing your technique for playing single notes, so they are an important part of your development as a guitar player.

We are going to learn the scale in the key of A, so, the A minor pentatonic scale. This is used to solo over a Blues or a song in the key of A minor, and we will be learning a 12-Bar Blues in the key of A very soon, so practise this scale now so you are ready to jam when we get to that.

Make sure you only pick one note at a time. Only use down-picks to start with; later, try to play using alternate picking (alternating between down and up picks).

The scale shape can be played on any fret, and the scale gets its name from the note under the R (root note).

To play it in the key of A—which is what you should do now—you should start with your 1st finger in the 5th fret.

For this scale, all the notes in the 5th fret are played using the 1st finger, all the notes in the 7th fret are played with the 3rd finger and all notes in the 8th fret are played with the 4th finger.

It is important that you get this scale 100% correct on the first few times you play it. You can only achieve this if you practise slowly enough to really get it right. Have a go at it now. Take it slowly enough to get it accurate. Don't start practising the wrong thing, there is no sense in that!

Play the notes in the order shown opposite.

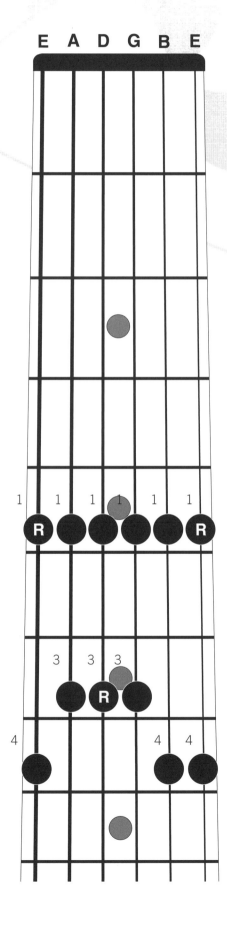

1.

```
T
A
B ———5———
     1
```

2.

```
T
A
B ———8———
     4
```

3.

```
T
A
B ———5———
     1
```

4.

```
T
A
B ———7———
     3
```

5.

```
T
A
B ———5———
     1
```

6.

```
T
A
B ———7———
     3
```

7.

```
T ———5———
A
B
     1
```

8.

```
T ———7———
A
B
     3
```

9.

```
T ———5———
A
B
     1
```

10.

```
T ———8———
A
B
     4
```

11.

```
  ———5———
T
A
B
     1
```

12.

```
  ———8———
T
A
B
     4
```

...and now play the same in reverse!

Here's the whole scale in tab:

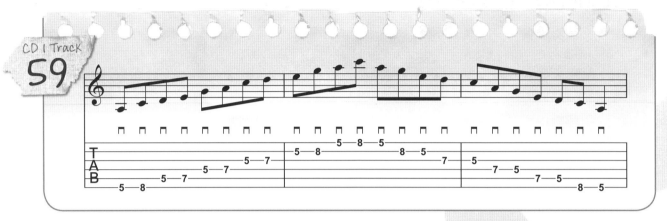

♻ Getting it right

Check that your fingers are not lifting far off the fingerboard. Try to keep all your finger movements small, and most importantly accurate.

Most guitarists use this scale, from Chuck Berry to Jimi Hendrix to Steve Vai. Learn this scale well and you will use it for the rest of your guitar playing days! So spend a bit of time with it and get it right.

If you can get to alternate picking this scale you should notice that all the notes fretted with your 1st finger will be picked with a down-pick and the rest with an up-pick. It's an easy way to check that you are doing it right!

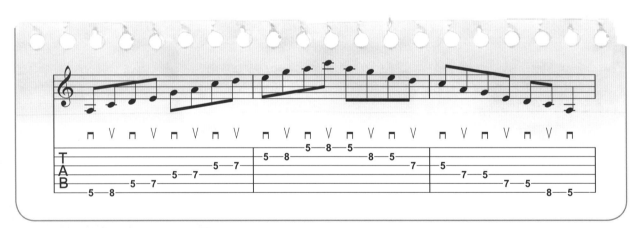

Use a metronome and play along with it, one note with each click. Try around 50bpm to start with, playing one note for every two clicks if you need to. Try and speed it up, gradually making it faster. When you get to 160bpm, cut it down to 80bpm and then do twice as many picks on each metronome click, and slowly work up the tempo.

Once you have it comfortably under your fingers, feel free to move it up and down the neck. See the little R on the scale diagram? That's the root note, and as with power chords, where you put that note decides the name of the scale. For instance, if you play the scale starting with your 1st finger in the 10th fret you'll be playing a D minor pentatonic. Cool, huh?

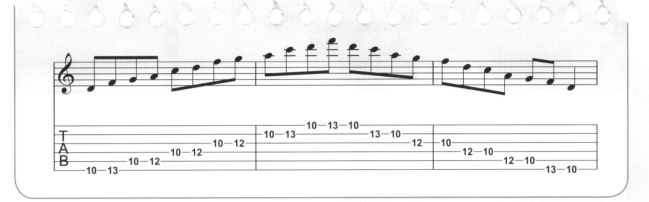

If you start on the thickest open E string, you can still use the same pattern; it's just that every other note is an open string:

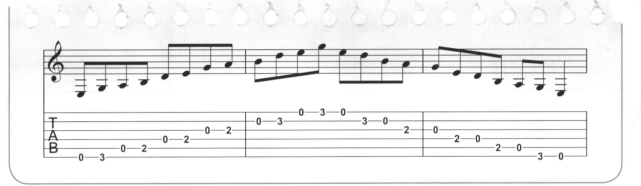

Fingerstyle (no pick) players can either use only the thumb (like Wes Montgomery), alternate between your first and 2nd fingers (like Segovia) or a mixture of thumb and fingers (like Jeff Beck). It's really up to you. I really do recommend learning to use a pick as well for this kind of thing, but if you really don't get along with them then you'll have to experiment a bit. There is such a thing as a thumb pick too which many fingerstyle players use that works like a pick (check out Chet Atkins and Tommy Emmanuel).

This scale is awesome for learning to improvise blues lead guitar over a 12-Bar blues sequence, which is coming up in Stage 8. For the time being, get working on this, try and get it smooth and memorise it so you're ready to go when we get to that.

J.U.S.T.I.N. Training Exercises

Chord Quality Recognition

Now we continue on from the last stage, just working on the same three qualities. Take it slow, and really focus on the quality of the chord. I am now playing each chord four times, and am playing them a little faster too. Really try and feel the character of the chord, I think of them as having a personality, so in these you are trying to get to know them better!

By the way, by this stage, you should be trying to complete the CQR exercises without needing your guitar!

CD 1 Track **60**

Sound Palette: major or minor or 7

		Attempt 1	Attempt 2	Attempt 3	Attempt 4
CHORD	1.				
	2.				
	3.				
	4.				
	5.				
	6.				
	7.				
	8.				
	9.				
	10.				

Single Sound Recognition

Many choices…I hope you are getting the hang of this now…

CD 1 Track 61

Chord Palette: E, A, D, Em, Am, Dm, G, C, G7, C7, B7, D7, E7, A7, Fmaj7, F

CHORD		Attempt 1	Attempt 2	Attempt 3	Attempt 4
	1.				
	2.				
	3.				
	4.				
	5.				
	6.				
	7.				
	8.				
	9.				
	10.				

Chord Progression Recognition

As in the last few stages, I will be playing the chords for either two or four strums. Off you go… sometimes I might stay on a chord a little longer, so keep an ear out!

CD 1 Track 62

Chord Palette: E, A, D, Em, Am, Dm, G, C, G7, C7, B7, D7, E7, A7, Fmaj7, F

BAR		1.	2.	3.	4.
EXERCISE	1.				
	2.				
	3.				

As ever, there's answers for these on page 140, but you don't need them, do you?

Getting Started

Stage 1

Stage 2

Stage 3

Stage 4

Stage 5

Stage 6

Stage 7

Stage 8

Stage 9

Bonus

We're up to 40-minute routine now!

As usual, break it into two 20-minute sessions if you can't find time to do 40 minutes a day. That is quite a lot of work for a beginner, but you will see results pretty quickly once you start putting that much time in!

Sometimes it can help to muck around for 5–10 minutes first to get your hands warmed up a bit. When I practise I usually spend 10 minutes just playing whatever comes to mind. It's not a proper warm up like I see some people doing, but gets my fingers ready for the coming aerobics…

Things to remember

Notes In The Open Position

Work out the notes in your open chords, or randomly pick notes in the first five frets and then try and work out what the note is. Only two minutes' worth, but if you do it every practice session you will soon have it!

Memorising The Notes On The Sixth String

This one is VERY IMPORTANT. You will use this information in lots of different ways. You need it for your power chords now, and you will use it for all your scales and eventually barre chords, so don't skip this!

The Minor Pentatonic Scale

You need to get this into your memory and it is also great practice for individual note picking and also works your finger stretch and independence. Do it slow and get it right!

Power Chords

Work on the stretch and getting the thin strings muted. We'll be developing these chords in the next stage, so make sure you are comfortable with these before you move on.

Chord sequences to try

The first two progressions here are to be played with power chords with a sixth-string root.

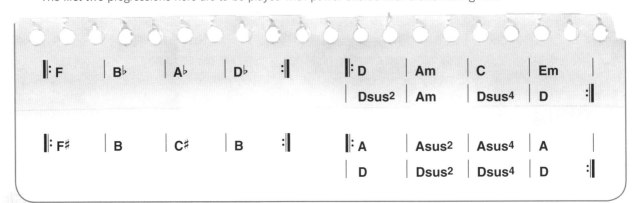

Stage 7 Practice chart (40 minutes)

Start date: _____

Work	Details	Time	M	T	W	T	F	S	S
Note Names	From memory: name all the notes in the open position and the notes of the chords you know so far.	00:02:00							
	Name the notes on the sixth (thickest) string	00:02:00							
Minor Pentatonic Scale	Practise and memorize	00:05:00							
Chord Practice	Asus4	00:01:00							
	Asus2	00:01:00							
	Dsus4	00:01:00							
	Dsus4	00:01:00							
	Esus4	00:01:00							
One-Minute Changes (write in how many changes you did each day)	D/Dm to Dsus4/Dsus2	00:01:00							
	A/Am to Asus4/Asus2	00:01:00							
	F to ?	00:01:00							
	F to ?	00:01:00							
	F to ?	00:01:00							
Power Chords	Stretching etc.	00:05:00							
Rhythm Guitar	All patterns so far	00:05:00							
Songs/Chord Sequences (write in details each day)		00:05:00							
J.U.S.T.I.N. Training	Chord Quality Recognition	00:02:00							
	Single Sound Recognition	00:02:00							
	Chord Progression Recognition	00:02:00							

Getting Started · Stage 1 · Stage 2 · Stage 3 · Stage 4 · Stage 5 · Stage 6 · Stage 7 · Stage 8 · Stage 9 · Bonus

Introduction

We're through the majority of the really basic stuff now, and we're starting to look at some really cool things to help your playing develop and set you up to grow in the future. We're going to check out some variations on the way you play a G chord that are commonly used and can really help speed up your changes. We're going to check out a classic 12-Bar blues shuffle riff, which sounds great and is the foundation for hundreds (if not thousands) of songs... so learn this and you instantly have a big repertoire!

We're also going to be looking at developing your technique a bit, doing some really basic fingerstyle (finger picking) patterns to get your strumming hand fingers used to the idea of working too, and further development of your single note picking (with the pick).

We're also going to look at power chords with a fifth string root note, so you will be able to play each power chord in two places on the neck, which means you don't have to move your hand so far or stare at the neck as much (there are usually nicer things to look at in the front row!).

BC-177

Here is a list of 10 songs—all included in the Justinguitar.com Beginner's Songbook—which you can play using the chords you'll know by the end of this stage:

Hallelujah (Leonard Cohen)

Fast Car (Tracy Chapman)

Fields Of Gold (Sting)

Vincent (Don McLean)

Wonderwall (Oasis)

Polly (Nirvana)

Molly's Chambers (Kings Of Leon)

The Sound Of Silence (Simon & Garfunkel)

All The Small Things (Blink-182)

Pretty Fly (For A White Guy) (The Offspring)

'Big', 'Rock' and 'Folk'

Now you have done some hard stretches, I'll show you some little tricks to speed up your changes to and from G. It is up to you where you might use all this, but I'll offer you some suggestions. The names below are how I describe these chords; they're not official or anything!

'Big' G

Otherwise known as 'all-finger G', this chord is used a lot by rock bands when they play acoustic songs, especially those early 90s groups like Guns n' Roses, Bon Jovi, Extreme etc. Both this chord and the one below change very smoothly to a D chord using a 3rd finger anchor. However, this one can sound a bit messy if you use distortion.

CD 2 Track 1

G

'Rock' G

This shape removes the note B so really it is a kind of G5 chord (it only has G and D notes; the 3rd of the chord is missing). This one sounds great with a bit of distortion. I use this G a lot because I don't like the sound of the B note; it just kind of makes the sound muddy to me. This one is used by bands like AC/DC, it really rocks!

CD 2 Track 2

G5

Getting Started

Stage 1

Stage 2

Stage 3

Stage 4

Stage 5

Stage 6

Stage 7

Stage 8

Stage 9

Bonus

'Folk' G

This shape changes very smoothly from a C Chord; the 2nd and 3rd finger moves over and little finger goes down. Try for yourself and see. I often let my 3rd finger mute the fifth string—that note usually sounds muddy, anyway—so I am only using two fingers (the 3rd and the 4th), which I think sounds cool. Also, it's easier this way to move to and from other chords.

CD 2 Track **3**

G

A little extra tip for you... If you take 'Big' G and move your 1st and 2nd fingers down a string you end up with a really cool chord called Cadd9, which you can usually use instead of a C. It sounds awesome in songs like 'Knockin' On Heaven's Door' (Bob Dylan or Guns N' Roses), 'Wanted Dead Or Alive' (Bon Jovi), 'More Than

Words' (Extreme), 'Brown Eyed Girl' (Van Morrison) or 'American Pie' (Don McLean) and you'll find it very easy to change between 'Big' G, Cadd9 and D because you can use a 3rd finger anchor. You will find that you can usually play Cadd9 instead of a plain C written in a song, but you have to listen and let your ears decide if it's cool or not!

CD 2 Track **4** **Cadd⁹**

It's getting personal now!

Everybody struggles with different things! Part of the journey is learning how to teach yourself because there are many things ahead that are better figured out on your own, so make a start with choosing the chords you need to work on!

I would recommend putting some of the new G shapes in alongside work on any changes that you are still struggling with.

C to G ('folk' version)

D to G ('big' version)

? to ?

? to ?

? to ?

Getting Started

Stage 1

Stage 2

Stage 3

Stage 4

Stage 5

Stage 6

Stage 7

Stage 8

Stage 9

Bonus

Getting Started

Stage 1

Stage 2

Stage 3

Stage 4

Stage 5

Stage 6

Stage 7

Stage 8

Stage 9

Bonus

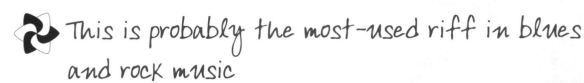

This is probably the most-used riff in blues and rock music

This blues riff is very important to learn! You'll hear this sequence in thousands of songs, either in this 'pure' form or with a couple of simple variations.

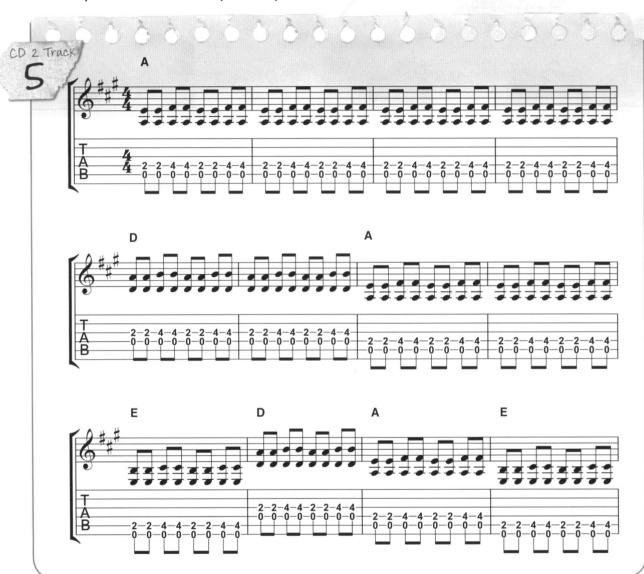

CD 2 Track 5

Start with your 1st finger in the 2nd fret (fourth string). Play this note, and the open fifth string together twice. Then, making sure you leave your 1st finger down the whole time, add your 3rd finger two frets higher and play those notes twice. So, the 3rd finger goes off and on the 4th fret (fourth string), while you also play the open fifth string.

Always play the string that has your finger on it and also the next thickest string (physically the string above it). None of the other strings should be played at all. Try and let your 1st finger rest on the strings below the note you are playing to mute them. Just a soft touch will be enough to stop them from ringing out.

Changing between the chords is the hardest part. It will be easier if you remember to always start a new chord with only your 1st finger down, and of course you will always finish a bar with the 3rd finger down. This gives you a chance to change the string that your 3rd finger is on, and will help make each transition smooth.

Take it slow to start with and make sure that you play the right amount of notes on each chord, otherwise it won't be a 12-Bar blues. It might help to count along with each bar, "1 + 2 + 3 + 4 +". If you can, try to tap your foot on beats 1, 2, 3 and 4.

Try and focus on maintaining an even rhythm as you change chords. This won't be easy at first, but you should get it after a few goes.

The rhythm was described to me when I learnt it as a 'Chunka-Chunka' rhythm (thanks to my first teacher in Tasmania, Peter Thompson!). The proper word is swing 8s or a shuffle. You should be able to get it by listening to the CD, or by saying "Chunka-Chunka" as you play, which might sound a bit silly but gives you the rhythm. We have already looked at the shuffle rhythm in BC-156 • Rhythm Guitar Basics #3 (Page 100), so this should be familiar.

Now some of you may notice that I am doing some string muting in the video on the website. Now, to tell the truth, I shouldn't have been, because it's a more advanced technique than you should be thinking about now, but because a few people asked about it in the forum I'm adding this in.

The picking hand has a few jobs going on; it sometimes does a palm mute, or a partial mute, but to get a real distinctive shuffle it also does a full mute between each pair of notes (on the 'trip' of the triplet count). So, it goes note, mute, note note, mute, note note, mute, note note etc. I really do not recommend you getting into doing that yet! Maybe have a try if you are feeling 100% confident with the normal playing, but it's not something a beginner should focus on. There's more about palm muting in Stage 9.

 ## Listening and onwards...

You should really concentrate on getting a good feel for this kind of riff, and so you need to hear how this kind of playing should sound. Listen to some old Chuck Berry, Status Quo or Rolling Stones songs for great examples of this. Spend a bit of time with the blues before you move on. It is the basis for a great many songs so it is an important thing to have in your repertoire.

You must really get this sorted before you move onto the next stage, because it builds on what you have been doing here and if you have not got it down you'll find the next part will be very difficult.

Getting Started

Stage 1

Stage 2

Stage 3

Stage 4

Stage 5

Stage 6

Stage 7

Stage 8

Stage 9

Bonus

Playing without a pick

In this exercise you will place your fingers on strings 1, 2 and 3, with your 1st finger plucking the 3rd string, 2nd finger plucking the 2nd string and 3rd finger plucking the 1st string. Your thumb will alternate between the sixth, fifth and fourth strings.

This is just an exercise to get your fingers working. We'll put them into proper patterns in the next stage!

CD 2 Track **6**

People with a long enough little finger use it as an anchor near the edge of the soundhole (on an acoustic guitar), and this helps keep the fingers in the right place. My little finger is too short to do this and though I would love to use this anchor the rest of my fingers are just too cramped if I do. So I have to 'float'. It makes finger picking a bit harder but with practice you will be able to judge where the strings are and get your hand to stay in roughly the same place. If you do have a long enough little finger I would recommend using the anchor technique, the vast majority of great fingerstyle players use it!

As you may have noticed, I use fake nails (acrylic or gel) because I play guitar a lot, and my natural nails would just wear out with all the playing I do. But I think I like the sound of natural nails a bit better. It is 100% totally fine to use the flesh of your finger tips, too. The great guitar player Dominic Miller (who plays with Sting and as a solo artist) told me once he was cutting his nails and

using flesh because it sounds better, and it sure works for him because his sound is amazing. So if you have nails, look after them and use them. If not, be happy to use the flesh, it will be fine.

Getting the volume consistent for each note is one of the hardest things to learn when playing fingerstyle so don't get discouraged if your notes are all unevenly loud of soft. Sometimes you will find that one finger seems to be making one of the strings too loud. The remedy for this is much more likely to be simple practice than any kind of complicated technical issue.

A very cool exercise you can do once you are getting all the right strings confidently is to do the above exercises, but focusing purely on volume. Try to play as loud as you can for a few times through, and then as soft as you can for a while. You will almost certainly notice that you start missing notes. It's very good practice but don't stress about it too much, because it's pretty tricky!

Fingers 1, 2, and 3 on the top three strings. In this example my thumb is picking the fifth string.

Getting Started

Stage 1

Stage 2

Stage 3

Stage 4

Stage 5

Stage 6

Stage 7

Stage 8

Stage 9

Bonus

 ## Developing your picking technique

This lesson is all about developing your picking skills in a useful way that will help you learn your minor pentatonic scales as well. You should try doing it free time (try and tap your foot if you can!) first, and make sure you are doing it right. As soon as you are, you should put on the metronome and play along, and then slowly speed the tempo up! These exercises are all shown for the A Minor Pentatonic Scale.

 ## The exercise

Play the Minor Pentatonic Scale with:

 ## All down-picks

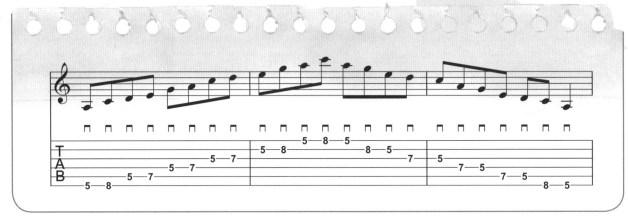

All up-picks

Yes, most people find this a bit tricky!

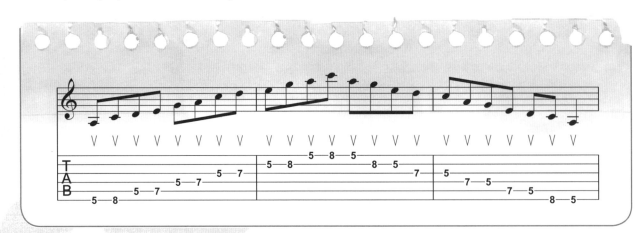

148

Down and up-pick on each note

Each note will be played twice.

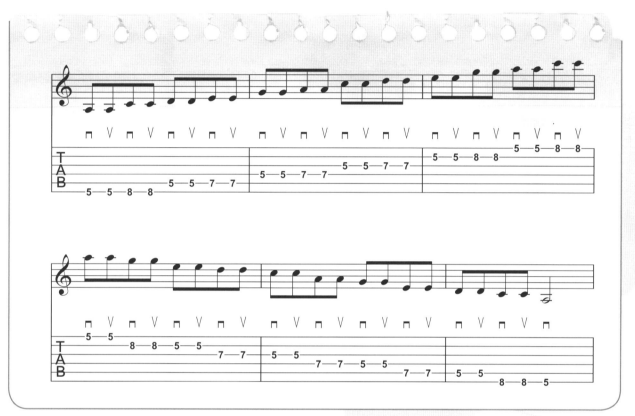

Alternate picking

Down with the 1st finger notes and up with all the rest.

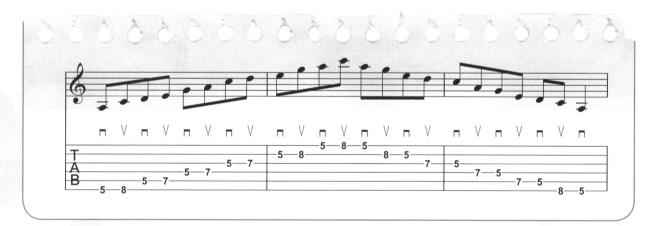

Getting Started

Stage 1

Stage 2

Stage 3

Stage 4

Stage 5

Stage 6

Stage 7

Stage 8

Stage 9

Bonus

Getting Started

Stage 1

Stage 2

Stage 3

Stage 4

Stage 5

Stage 6

Stage 7

Stage 8

Stage 9

Bonus

...and then there were two root notes

Once you have got those sixth-string root power chords down, we can get in to playing chords with a fifth-string root. The principle is exactly the same, but the notes are different of course, and there is an additional technique needed.

Use only your 1st, 3rd and 4th fingers as shown, and start by putting your 1st finger in the 3rd fret of the fifth string (the note C). Then put down your 3rd and 4th fingers. If this is a bit of stretch don't worry, you will soon limber up! Try to keep them together, the 3rd finger sort of on top of the 4th as shown below.

CD 2 Track **7**

C5

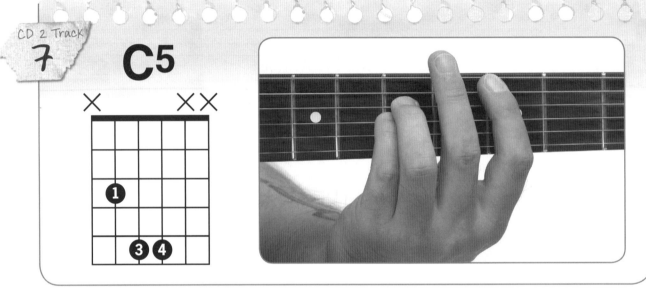

This is what the chord should look like, with the 1st finger muting the two thinnest strings.

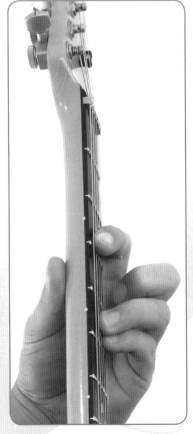

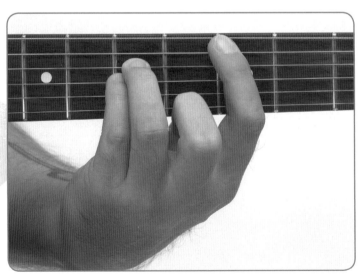

Here it is with the 2nd finger moved out of the way to show exactly which strings are being fretted.

Now you have to mute the sixth string!

Notice that the sixth string must not be played. A power chord with its root on the fifth string will sound very bad indeed if you forget to mute this string. So how do you do that?

Well we use our 1st finger—the very tip—to press on the side of the sixth string. Not hard enough to make the note sound, but hard enough to stop the note ringing out. See the photo and try and copy my hand position.

Some people use the middle finger to help mute the sixth string. It's O.K. to do this, but you still have to mute with the 1st finger too!

See how the tip of my 1st finger is very lightly touching the sixth string.

Getting Started

Stage 1

Stage 2

Stage 3

Stage 4

Stage 5

Stage 6

Stage 7

Stage 8

Stage 9

Bonus

151

Getting Started

Stage 1

Stage 2

Stage 3

Stage 4

Stage 5

Stage 6

Stage 7

Stage 8

Stage 9

Bonus

Two ways to play

Every power chord can be played in two places in the neck, and this means you've got a choice of position to play the chord. For instance, look at this chord progression (you might recognise it!):

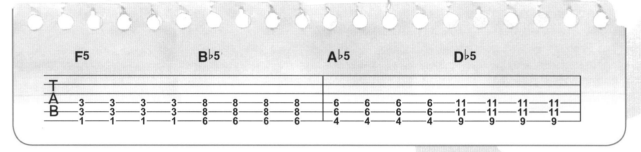

You've got to make some big leaps to get some of the notes, right? Shooting up the neck from the

4th fret to the 9th is tricky. Well, now look at this example:

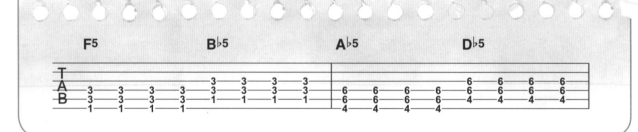

These are the same chords, but changing position makes the whole sequence easier; moving across the strings instead of up and down the neck.

So if you look closely now at the neck diagram opposite you can see that there are now two ways of playing every power chord; one with the sixth-string root and one with a fifth-string root! For example, you could play C5 with the root on the

8th fret, sixth string, or the same chord on the 3rd fret, fifth string.

You will have to learn how to figure out which one you should use when. Use a little logic, and listen. Sometimes it is better to play them all on one string anyway, because the sound will stay consistent. Use your ears and your head!

Now check out some tunes!

The best way to learn these chrds is to put them into practice and learn some songs! There are some in the songbook, and more listed on the website, but what I really recommend is this:

On the website in the 'Transcribing' area you will find a lesson called TR-201 • Listening To The Bass Note which is all about working out power chord songs, just by using your ear! This is by far the best way to learn songs, and in this lesson I give you lots of tips so that you can develop your listening skills as well as your playing and repertoire. There are loads of great songs out there:

Song 2 (Blur)
Teenage Kicks (Undertones)
Polly (Nirvana)
Basket Case (Green Day)
Hate To Say I Told You So (The Hives)
All The Small Things (Blink-182)
Pretty Fly (For A White Guy) (The Offspring)
Seven Nation Army (The White Stripes)

...and many, many more.

Once you develop this skill you will find you can work out songs on your own, and that is a great feeling; no longer do you need to rely on dodgy internet tabs (which are usually wrong anyway). You can do it yourself, and know that it's right!!

It can be tricky. You might find that reading the other articles on transcribing will help too. It's such a valuable skill that it's worth a little pain and frustration!

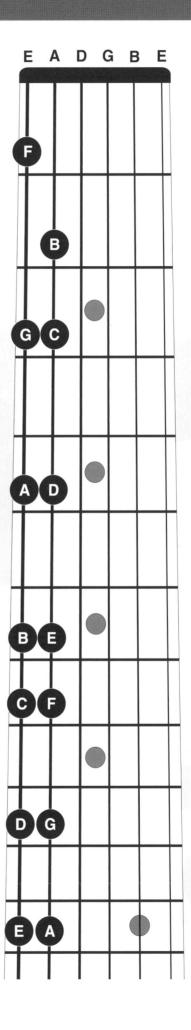

Getting Started
Stage 1
Stage 2
Stage 3
Stage 4
Stage 5
Stage 6
Stage 7
Stage 8
Stage 9
Bonus

Chord Quality Recognition

We are now including power chords in this test. They should stand out because they sound a little different from open chords. Remember, you write power chords as just '5', because they only consist of a root note and a note a 5th above it. I'm also including a maj7 chord for you to spot.

CD 2 Track **8**

Sound Palette: major, minor, 7, maj7 and power chords (5).

CHORD		Attempt 1	Attempt 2	Attempt 3	Attempt 4
	1.				
	2.				
	3.				
	4.				
	5.				
	6.				
	7.				
	8.				
	9.				
	10.				

Single Sound Recognition

In this stage, we are only looking at power chords. The task now is to find the root note! Let the chord play and then pause and try to keep the sound in your ear, and then move your power chord shape up and down the neck until you find the right root note. You may have to rewind a few times, but that is O.K.

CD 2 Track
9

Chord Palette: All power chords, from any root note, with either a fifth or sixth string root.

		Attempt 1	Attempt 2	Attempt 3	Attempt 4
CHORD	1.				
	2.				
	3.				
	4.				
	5.				
	6.				
	7.				
	8.				
	9.				
	10.				

Chord Progression Recognition

In this stage we're just looking at power chord progressions. If you get through this O.K., then you should start trying to work out some rock songs by yourself; it is a lot easier than you might think. Of course it takes some practice, but your ears should be developing nicely by now!

I will be doing either 2 or 4 strums on each chord. Listen up! These are all power chords!

CD 2 Track
10

Chord Palette: All power chords, from any root note, with either a fifth or sixth string root.

BAR		1.	2.	3.	4.
EXERCISE	1.				
	2.				
	3.				

As ever, there's answers for these on page 159, but you're not going to need them, are you?

Getting Started
Stage 1
Stage 2
Stage 3
Stage 4
Stage 5
Stage 6
Stage 7
Stage 8
Stage 9
Bonus

Getting Started

Stage 1

Stage 2

Stage 3

Stage 4

Stage 5

Stage 6

Stage 7

Stage 8

Stage 9

Bonus

 ## We're up to a 50-minute practice session now!

This is quite a lot of practice, so divide it into two sessions if you need to. Some of this (like learning the note names) is purely mental, so you can do this while you are on the train or the bus or while you are having dinner if you like, as you don't need your guitar. Practising in your 'dead time' is something you can do a lot of. I spent a lot of time doing 'mental' practice; strumming in the air, imagining doing my chord changes and trying to mentally picture the notes on the fingerboard, so you might like to try that too!

 ## Things to remember

Memorising Notes On The Fifth and Sixth Strings

This is VERY IMPORTANT. You will use this information in lots of different ways; you need it for your power chords now, and you will use it for all your scales and eventually your barre chords, so don't skip this! Once you have learnt the notes on these two strings it is easy to work out the other notes all over the neck as well.

Minor Pentatonic Practice

You need to memorize this. This scale is also great practice for individual note picking and also develops your finger stretch and independence. Do it slow and get it right! You should also be working a bit on the picking exercises too. We will start to look at using it in the next stage so try and get it under your fingers as best you can!

Power Chords

Work on stretching for these chords and keeping the thin strings muted. We've now got them on two strings, so you need to practise both, with an emphasis on muting the sixth string with the tip of your finger when you are playing the fifth-string root chords.

Rhythm Guitar Practice

Spend your time playing the patterns over and over again. Practise your strumming patterns with songs or chord sequences, but only if you can do it without stopping between the chords.

12-Bar Blues

Just try to keep this pattern in time and play it all the way through without stopping. Don't forget that playing this very slowly makes it sound cool, as well as giving you time to get it right, so don't be afraid to play it slow!

Basic Fingerstyle

If you have not done any fingerstyle before you might find this a little tricky, so don't be in a hurry. Allow yourself time to develop these new motor skills!

Stage 8 Practice chart (50 minutes)

Start date: _____

Work	Details	Time	M	T	W	T	F	S	S
Note Names	From memory: name all the notes on the thickest two strings (sixth and fifth)	00:05:00							
Minor Pentatonic Scale	Practise and memorize	00:05:00							
Chord Practice	'Big' G	00:01:00							
	'Rock' G	00:01:00							
	'Folk' G	00:01:00							
	Pick a chord that needs work!	00:01:00							
One-Minute Changes (write in how many changes you did each day)	C to 'Big' G	00:01:00							
	'Big' G to D	00:01:00							
	? to ?	00:01:00							
	? to ?	00:01:00							
	? to ?	00:01:00							
Power Chords	Shapes on the fifth string	00:05:00							
Rhythm Guitar	All patterns so far, including RUST #16	00:05:00							
12-Bar Blues Style Rhythm		00:05:00							
Basic Fingerstyle Practice		00:05:00							
Songs/Chord Sequences (write in details each day)		00:05:00							
J.U.S.T.I.N. Training	Chord Quality Recognition	00:02:00							
	Single Sound Recognition	00:02:00							
	Chord Progression Recognition	00:02:00							

Getting Started
Stage 1
Stage 2
Stage 3
Stage 4
Stage 5
Stage 6
Stage 7
Stage 8
Stage 9
Bonus

Stage 9

Getting Started

Stage 1

Stage 2

Stage 3

Stage 4

Stage 5

Stage 6

Stage 7

Stage 8

Stage 9

Bonus

 ## Introduction

Well done you! I hope you are really enjoying all this so far. Now we're going to introduce some cool things for you to develop in the future!

Learning guitar is a never-ending journey and I still practise and learn new stuff almost every day!

Consolidation is the most important thing for you at this stage. Before even thinking about moving onto the Intermediate Course, you should spend 6–12 months developing the skills you have learned here. If you can play all the stuff in this book really well, you will be good enough to perform live. In fact, I know some big-name pop stars who don't know any more guitar skills than those covered in this book!

So don't rush, enjoy the ride and play songs you like. There's nothing wrong with learning some new bits here and there—some new chords or exploring strumming or theory and things like that—but in my experience the people that spend time making these basic skills really solid before going further have the best ride; they struggle less when learning barre chords, and they understand the value of practice!

BC-197

Here is a list of 10 songs—all included in the Justinguitar.com Beginner's Songbook—which you can play using the chords we've covered in this course.

Better Be Home Soon (Crowded House)

Have You Ever Seen The Rain (Creedence Clearwater Revival)

Wherever You Will Go (The Calling)

American Pie (Don McLean)

Redemption Song (Bob Marley & The Wailers)

Wonderful Tonight (Eric Clapton)

Don't Think Twice, It's All Right (Bob Dylan)

Zombie (The Cranberries)

Hand In My Pocket (Alanis Morissette)

Let It Be (The Beatles)

J.U.S.T.I.N. TEST ANSWERS FOR STAGE 8

THE ANSWERS! NO PEEKING...
CQR: 1) Am 2) B7 3) G5 4) C (maj)
5) D (maj) 6) C5 7) D7 8) Fmaj7 9) G7
10) A (maj)
SSR: 1) G5 2) C5 3) D5 4) F5 5) E5
6) A#5 7) C#5 8) F#5 9) A#5 10) D#5

CPR:	BAR:	1.	2.	3.	4.
EXERCISE	1.	C5	G5	F5	G5
	2.	D5	C5	F5 G5	A5
	3.	F5 B♭5	A♭5 D♭5	F5 B♭5	A♭5 D♭5

159

Getting Started

Stage 1

Stage 2

Stage 3

Stage 4

Stage 5

Stage 6

Stage 7

Stage 8

Stage 9

Bonus

 Slash chords have nothing to do with the guitarist from Guns n' Roses.

Slash chords simply have a different note at the bass of the chord than the shapes we've seen so far.

D/F#

This is a lovely chord to place between a G and an Em, and you'll often hear that progression. 'Better Man' by Pearl Jam uses this chord a lot, as does Pink Floyd's 'Wish You Were Here'.

The bass note is usually played with the thumb grabbing over the neck, but if you struggle with this (I couldn't do it for years!) then re-finger the chord. Use your 1st finger on the bass note and use fingers 2/3/4 on the rest of the chord. Some people use a small mini-barre on the D Chord if they use the thumb on the bass, which I don't think is a great idea but it's not going to cause any problems that I can think of!

It's fine for the A (fifth) string to sound as part of this chord. I usually think it sounds better to mute it (with the thumb). A is a note in the chord of D, so it certainly won't sound wrong, but I just hear it making it sound a little too full, or muddy.

CD 2 Track 11 — D/F#

G/B

This chord is used more for 'joining' C and Am than on its own.

C/G

This version of C is proper 'old skool!' I love the sound of the bass note and often replace a regular C chord with this, just because it sounds great, but you have to let YOUR ears be the judge, not mine. There are two variations on this chord shown here.

CD 2 Track
12 G/B

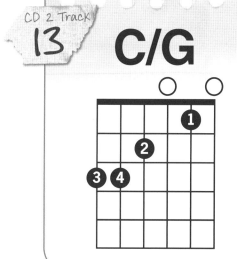

CD 2 Track
13 C/G

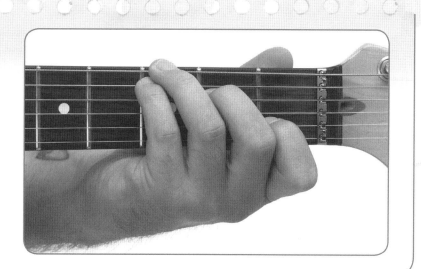

CD 2 Track
14 C/G

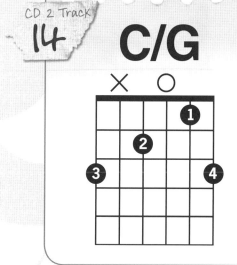
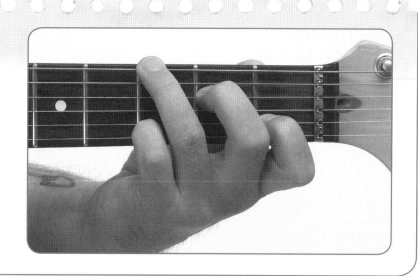

Power Chord Shifts And Palm Mutes

Getting Started

Stage 1

Stage 2

Stage 3

Stage 4

Stage 5

Stage 6

Stage 7

Stage 8

Stage 9

Bonus

 You have the basics down, but if you really wanna rock then you have to master another couple of tricks...

Have another look at the chord sequence on page 152 and experiment with shifting between chords.

 ## Shifting power chords with a little lift

Moving power chords around should be easy, and it is if you use this little trick. What you want to do is keep the fingers in contact with the strings all the time when you change chord. Don't lift all your fingers off and replace them each time, because it's far too much wasted effort. The chord grip stays the same all the time, so it should be easy, right?

So what I recommend you try is moving your power chord grip from, say, a G up to a B (6th string root) and try and make sure that your hand shape stays the same, and that the fingers never leave the strings. However, don't keep pressing hard or you will hear a really strange sound while you slide the chord up. The trick is to play the first chord, and then when it's time to shift the chord

you relax your fingers while keeping them in the right place. Leave them lightly touching the strings and then shift to the place for the new chord, press hard again and then play.

If you press too hard you will find that the friction of the strings will move your fingers out of the correct chord form, and if you press too lightly or remove your fingers you will get open string noise (and when using distortion the noise becomes significantly greater).

This is easier said than done, but it shouldn't take you much practice, and it will really improve the sound of your power chord songs!

 CD 2 Track **15**

 ## Palm muting

The outside of your picking hand palm will rest on the edge of the bridge and lightly mute the strings so they sound a little dead. Makes it more of a 'chug' sound than a 'ringing out' sound, that sounds especially good with a distorted tone.

You have to experiment with exactly where to put your palm down, that is, how far away from the bridge to rest it. If you're sat exactly on the bridge, then the effect will not be noticeable, but if you're too far towards the neck, the strings will be so dead you won't hear any note at all, just a click! In practice you'll choose different positions depending on what you are playing, the song, the style, and your mood.

Chug, chug, chug...

Ditch the pick!

Now we have to work on some patterns to apply to work out which strings to play for which chord...

Your thumb always plays the bass note. It can play other notes later of course, but for these patterns the thumb will always play the bass note of the chord. Now you do remember the notes in your chords way back when we looked at notes in the open position, right? Two patterns with four beats in each bar are shown below:

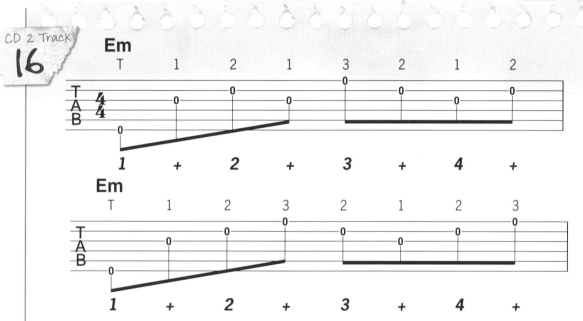

CD 2 Track **16**

And one more, which is has six beats in the bar. Now, we have not looked at that timing yet, but you can think of it like a half bar (2 beats) with each beat divided into 3 (triplets). Many people (including me when I was learning) use it to play 'House Of The Rising Sun', but the original uses a slightly different rhythm and is actually played with a pick.

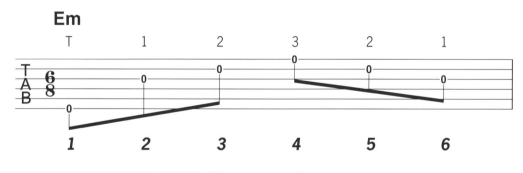

Make up your own!

In a bar with four beats there are eight eighth notes (1+2+3+4+). Now, if you put a bass note on beat 1, then you can make up any other pattern you like for the other fingers. It will usually sound better if the pattern is the same in each bar, but sometimes it sounds cool just to make them all up as you go! Try right now to make up your own eight-note fingerstyle pattern and then play it. It's easy and lots of fun, and will teach you heaps of cool new patterns!

It might seem sometimes that you have more fingers pressing down notes in the chord than you really need. But leave them there because if you accidentally hit the wrong string (which often happens) then at least it will be a good note. Holding down the whole chord is a great habit to get into. When you are a fingerstyle expert you might not hold them all down all the time, but until then, it will keep you sounding cool.

Getting Started

Stage 1

Stage 2

Stage 3

Stage 4

Stage 5

Stage 6

Stage 7

Stage 8

Stage 9

Bonus

Introduction

Once you've mastered the basic 12-Bar Blues rhythm it is time to move onto using variations on the basic pattern, allowing you to improvise within the rhythm part. This is great fun and pretty easy.

Basic pattern

You should have this down from the work you did in the last stage (page 144) If you haven't, here's a reminder:

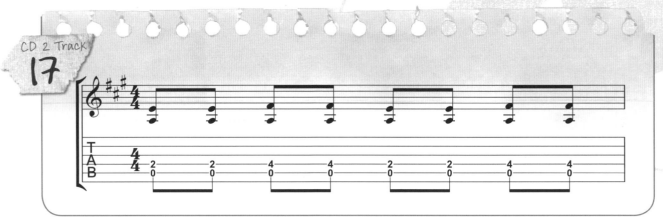

CD 2 Track 17

Variation 1

This variation only changes the two notes on beats 3 +. Reach out and play them with your little finger. Make sure you leave your 1st finger down in the right place; don't let it slip up.

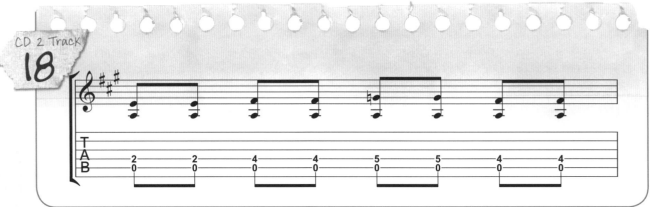

CD 2 Track 18

Variation 2

This one introduces using the 2nd and 3rd fingers on the fifth string, a kind of bass effect. Make sure you pick the right notes; try to keep it clean, and don't pick strings that you shouldn't.

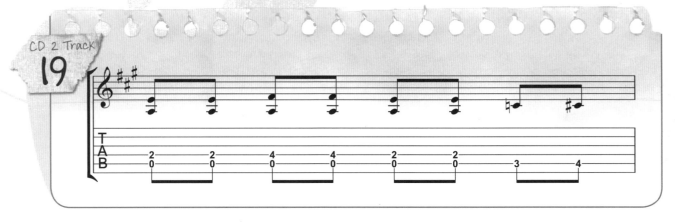

CD 2 Track 19

Variation 3

This is a mixture of the previous examples.

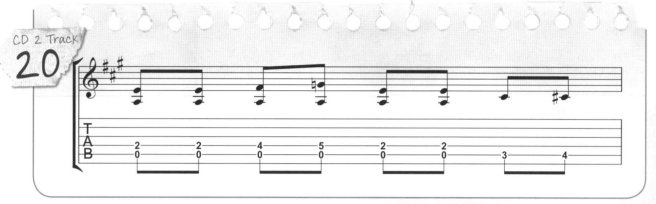

CD 2 Track
20

Variation 4

This is another variation on the above patterns. Try this one, then try to make up your own!!.

CD 2 Track
21

D.I.Y.

It's important that you try to make up your own patterns. The only rule: make it sound cool! So experiment, twist and turn these patterns, listen out for variations on recordings and try to copy them.

You might have noticed too that in the video for this lesson I am sometimes using a palm mute (see page 162) between some of the notes to keep them short. As you progress you can have a go at this and see if you can get your hand to do it. I'm just using the outside palm of my picking hand. The trick is not to think about the technique too much and just try and make your guitar make the sound you want and leave it up to your hand to sort out the technicalities!

Getting Started

Stage 1

Stage 2

Stage 3

Stage 4

Stage 5

Stage 6

Stage 7

Stage 8

Stage 9

Bonus

Getting Started

Stage 1

Stage 2

Stage 3

Stage 4

Stage 5

Stage 6

Stage 7

Stage 8

Stage 9

Bonus

Mixing scales and maths... yeah, great fun this, Justin!

If you practise playing scales a lot, it is likely that your muscle memory will limit you to playing up and down the scale when you improvise. Using melodic patterns to train your fingers to play the notes in different orders will help you get to know the scale really well. Picking should be alternate picking the whole way through. I know at some points it seems kind of tricky but as you speed up you really want your alternate picking to be able to handle small jumps and complicated patterns!

Three-in-a-line

This pattern plays up three notes of the scale at a time, starting on each scale degree. If you numbered the scale you would end up with the sequence: 1,2,3—2,3,4—3,4,5—4,5,6—5,6,7 etc.

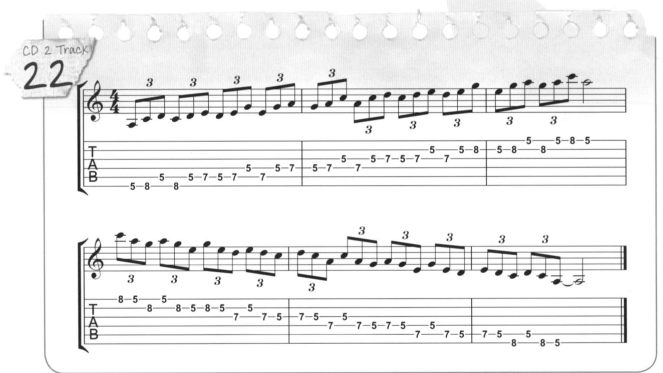

CD 2 Track
22

Loose 4ths

The pattern here is: play one note, miss one and play the next, then play the one you missed… miss one and play the next, etc. If you numbered the scale you would end up with this number sequence: 1, 3, 2, 4, 3, 5, 4, 6, 5, 7, etc.

CD 2 Track
23

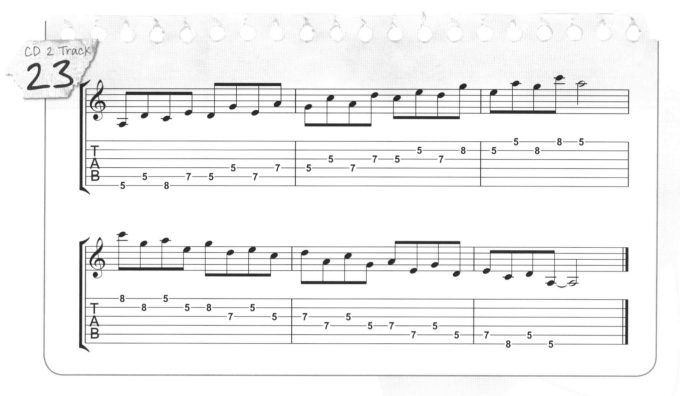

Getting Started

Stage 1

Stage 2

Stage 3

Stage 4

Stage 5

Stage 6

Stage 7

Stage 8

Stage 9

Bonus

 Now it's time to try and dip your toes into improvisation.

It might seem scary, but the more you improvise, the more comfortable you will feel about it. Many people wait way too long before giving it a go and then feel uncomfortable because they can play other stuff a lot better than they can improvise. It is great fun when you get into it, and I love watching people learning this, it's so cool when you realise that you can do it, the smile says it all!

So the best place to start with this is playing the A Minor Pentatonic Scale notes over the top of a 12-Bar Blues. The notes in the scale and the notes in the chords in the 12-Bar go really well together and there are no 'bad' notes so you can't go too wrong (if you play the right scale and stick to the scale notes). The chords for a 12-Bar Blues in A are shown below.

Start by playing the 12-Bar Blues backing track on your stereo or something loud enough so you can hear it while you play your guitar over the top (CD2

Track 48). Then place your first finger at the 5th fret of the thickest (sixth) string, and slowly play up the A Minor Pentatonic Scale (there's a reminder of this below). Make sure you listen to the sound of each note. Once you feel confident playing the scale up and down, try changing direction as you feel like it, or sometimes staying longer on one note, maybe playing some notes twice, just explore this idea.

At this stage you shouldn't be trying to sound like Eric Clapton; just be cool with having a go and not being scared. It might not sound great at first, but it will with some practice.

Improvising is something that takes time and practice and it's something you will most likely work on for many years, the long journey starts with a single step, and that's what I'd like you to take here. Stick at it a while and you are sure to start enjoying it. It's very rewarding once you can jam along with a friend or a playalong track!

‖: A7	A7	A7	A7	
D7	D7	A7	A7	
E7	D7	A7	E7	:‖

A 12-Bar Blues in A and the A Minor Pentatonic scale: all the ingredients you need to start improvising blues lead guitar.

Improv tips

Here are a few little tips to help you get get off to a good start:

Use space:

Be happy to leave a few bars silent and let your brain catch up. Eventually you don't really want to be thinking about what you are doing at all, but in the early stages you are going to have to!

Don't play too much.

Play a bit, then have a little rest, then play a bit more. Playing without any breaks sounds silly. Try and play how you speak, with punctuation and pauses for breath.

Keep it simple.

Many great players (e.g., B.B. King) play amazing solos using very few notes. Aim for that, not playing fast and doing flashy stuff. You are only learning. Remember: KISS. Keep It Simple, Stupid!

Listen!

Listen to what you play and what is going on around you (i.e., your backing track or the mate you are jamming with).

Learn from the masters.

The best way to learn what to do is listen to someone great! So, a lot of listening to your favourite blues guitar players will really help your ability to improvise; you will absorb some of the vocabulary just by listening.

The language.

Learning to improvise is like learning a language. We're starting by looking at the alphabet here—the scale—but soon you have to look at learning licks (words) and the putting licks together into phrases (sentences) and eventually writing some poetry! I teach all about licks and language in the Blues Lead Guitar course (which you can view for free on the website).

Timing is everything.

The thing that allows the masters to play amazing solos with just a few notes is that their sense of time is solid and they can manipulate it just the right way to touch our emotions. Pay attention to the timing of notes—not just what the notes are— and you will quickly develop your lead guitar skills.

Getting Started
Stage 1
Stage 2
Stage 3
Stage 4
Stage 5
Stage 6
Stage 7
Stage 8
Stage 9
Bonus

J.U.S.T.I.N. Training Exercises

Chord Quality Recognition

It's going to get a little tricky now, because we are going to include sus chords in this exercise. You will need to play these chords a lot on your own and really try to listen deeply. When you have listened a lot, they will become very obvious because they have a very distinctive sound!

CD 2 Track
24

Sound Palette: Major, Minor, 7, Maj7, power chords (5th) and sus chords.

CHORD	Attempt 1	Attempt 2	Attempt 3	Attempt 4
1.				
2.				
3.				
4.				
5.				
6.				
7.				
8.				
9.				
10.				

Single Sound Recognition

This exercise is also going to be tricky because we are including ALL chords we have covered so far in this course, so you have quite a few choices. Think of this as a little test. Can you do it?

CD 2 Track
25

Chord Palette: Every chord we have covered in this course, including slash chords and sus chords!

		Attempt 1	Attempt 2	Attempt 3	Attempt 4
CHORD	1.				
	2.				
	3.				
	4.				
	5.				
	6.				
	7.				
	8.				
	9.				
	10.				

Chord Progression Recognition

Now the progressions are a little longer: can you work them out? These are based on real songs. All I have done is remove the strumming patterns which are best studied separately. Good luck!

CD 2 Track
26

Chord Palette: Every chord we have covered in this course, including slash chords and sus chords!

1	Bar 1	Bar 2	Bar 3	Bar 4
	Bar 5	Bar 6	Bar 7	Bar 8
2	Bar 1	Bar 2	Bar 3	Bar 4
	Bar 5	Bar 6	Bar 7	Bar 8
3	Bar 1	Bar 2	Bar 3	Bar 4

As ever, there's answers for these on page 176, but you don't need them, do you?

Getting Started

Stage 1

Stage 2

Stage 3

Stage 4

Stage 5

Stage 6

Stage 7

Stage 8

Stage 9

Bonus

Getting Started
Stage 1
Stage 2
Stage 3
Stage 4
Stage 5
Stage 6
Stage 7
Stage 8
Stage 9
Bonus

 ## Well done!
You made it to the end—well—almost...

Now it's time to consolidate all you have learnt, so you are ready to go on with the next course, and get into the intermediate stage. So, use the chart (on page 174) to make sure that you feel confident with all the stuff we've covered in this course.

It is MUCH better to get really good at these things and be able to use them well to play some songs, than playing more advanced stuff badly. Really it is. Ask anyone that has to listen to you!

When you discover things that you don't know, make a list out of them and work out a practice schedule that gives each problem area a five-minute practice slot and then work on it until they are fixed. Then choose some more things to work on, until, eventually, you are on top of this whole list.

 ## Chords

You should instantly know ALL of the following chords and know any fingering variations for each that you can use, depending on the situation:

The basic eight shapes:
A, D, E, G, C, Am, Em, Dm.
The dominant shapes:
A7, D7, E7, G7, C7, B7.
The sus shapes:
Asus2, Asus4, Dsus2, Dsus4, Esus4.
F chord and variations:
F (three shapes), Fmaj7.
Basic slash chords:
D/F#, G/B, C/G.

You should be able to change between any two chords at a speed of 60 changes per minute (one change per second).

You should also be able to locate and play any power chord on either the fifth or sixth string and be able to play them without the open strings ringing out.

You should be familiar with some chord variations (for A and G and others) and know when you might use them.

Rhythms

You should be able to play RUST strumming patterns 1, 2, 4, 8, 9 and 16 confidently and fluently at a range of different tempi while tapping your foot.

You should also be able to play basic fingerstyle and be able to make to make up your own patterns.

 # Scales

You should know the minor pentatonic scale and be able to play it with one note per click with the metronome set at 120 beats per minute, using all down-picks, all up-picks and also alternate picking.

 # Improvising

You should be starting to experiment with using the minor pentatonic to improvise. Don't expect too much at this stage; just be able to play about and make up something easy over a blues.

Theory

You should understand and be able to use the following concepts:

- The note names of the open strings.
- Tones, semitones and the note circle.
- Sharps and flats.
- The names of all the notes in the first five frets of the guitar
- The principal elements of rhythm
- All the note names on the thickest two strings.
- How to use a capo.

 # Songs

You should be able to play at least ten songs all the way through without stopping. This might seem a lot, but it should be possible now with all the hard work you have done. The strumming should be solid too and you should be able to play in time with a metronome!

Getting Started

Stage 1

Stage 2

Stage 3

Stage 4

Stage 5

Stage 6

Stage 7

Stage 8

Stage 9

Bonus

Getting Started

Stage 1

Stage 2

Stage 3

Stage 4

Stage 5

Stage 6

Stage 7

Stage 8

Stage 9

Bonus

 ## Beginner's course consolidation chart

Work	Details	Page(s)	Completed
Chords	D	36	
	A	40	
	A with mini-barre	83	
	E	42	
	G	66	
	'Rock G'	141	
	'Big' G	141	
	'Folk' G	142	
	C	67	
	Am	54	
	Em	55	
	Dm	56	
	A7	94	
	D7	94	
	E7	95	
	E7 (with high D)	95	
	G7	80	
	C7	81	
	B7	82	
	Asus2	127	
	Asus4	126	
	Dsus2	128	
	Dsus4	128	
	Esus4	129	
	F (version 1)	108	
	F (version 2)	109	
	F (version 3)	109	
	Fmaj7	82	
	D/F#	160	
	G/B (version 1)	161	
	C/G (version 1)	161	
	C/G (version 2)	161	
	Cadd9	142	
Power Chords	All shapes with a root on sixth and fifth strings	123—125; 150—153	

Work	Details	Page(s)	Completed
Rhythms	RUST 1	72	
	RUST 2	72	
	RUST 4	86	
	RUST 8	87	
	RUST 9	114	
	RUST 16	131	
Basic Fingerstyle		146, 163	
Minor Pentatonic Scale	All down-picks, 120bpm	148	
	All up-picks, 120bpm	148	
	Alternate Picking, 120bpm	149	
Improvising	Using the minor pentatonic to improvise over a blues.	168—169	
Theory	Note names of the open strings	68	
	Tones, Semitones and the Note Circle	96	
	Sharps and flats	96	
	Note names in the first five frets of the guitar	122	
	Principal elements of rhythm	72	
	Note names on the sixth and fifth strings	153	
	Using a Capo	111	
Songs	At least 10 songs without stopping!		
	1.	—	
	2.	—	
	3.	—	
	4.	—	
	5.	—	
	6.	—	
	7.	—	
	8.	—	
	9.	—	
	10.	—	

Getting Started
Stage 1
Stage 2
Stage 3
Stage 4
Stage 5
Stage 6
Stage 7
Stage 8
Stage 9
Bonus

Getting Started

Stage 1

Stage 2

Stage 3

Stage 4

Stage 5

Stage 6

Stage 7

Stage 8

Stage 9

Bonus

Bonus Stage

Introduction

For this book I decided to add a little bonus content for you. This includes some things that have been very popular on the website and some further tools to help you develop your playing.

We've added a chord library with all the chords from the book alongside some of the other common open chords not covered in this course that you might find useful. There are many commonly used chords, but beware the books called things like '1 Gazillion Chords' as many of the chords are there to make up the numbers and are very rarely played in the real world. They may be very hard to play or just not sound good. Once you have mastered the chords in this book, you should move onto barre chords, which are found in my Intermediate Course, and then explore specialist chords that you might need depending on the style you want to play.

We've then got a guide for string changing (there are videos on the web site if you want to watch them!), and an article on getting a good sound from your amp, a full neck diagram showing all the notes on the neck and a capo chart.

To finish off I have included three songs to play: a simple 12-Bar Blues solo for you to play along with the backing track and then do some improvising with; a fingerstyle version of 'Silent Night', a great song for entertaining the family at Christmas and a great goal for all those of you that start playing around Christmas; can you complete the book and play that song in 12 months? Lastly, there is the imaginatively titled 'Solo Blues 1', a blues arrangement combining rhythm and lead guitar that has been extremely popular on YouTube and led to me making a DVD series of nine further similar songs.

Hope you enjoy it!

Here is a list of 10 more songs—all included in the Justinguitar.com Beginner's Songbook—which you can play now that you've gone through the whole course:

You're Beautiful (James Blunt)

Imagine (John Lennon)

Hey, Soul Sister (Train)

Wild World (Cat Stevens)

Use Somebody (Kings Of Leon)

Stuck In The Middle With You (Stealers Wheel)

Dream Catch Me (Newton Faulkner)

Substitute (The Who)

Driftwood (Travis)

Times Like These (Foo Fighters)

J.U.S.T.I.N. TEST ANSWERS FOR STAGE 9

THE ANSWERS! NO PEEKING...

CQR: 1) Em 2) Dsus4 3) F#5 4) C7
5) Fmaj7 6) G7 7) Asus2 8) B7 9) Fmaj7
10) Am
SSR: 1) G5 2) D/F# 3) D7 4) F 5) D5
6) Esus4 7) A7 8) Am 9) Dsus2 10) Fmaj7

CPR:
1) You just worked out verse to 'Wish You Were Here' by Pink Floyd!
2) You just worked out the chord progression to 'Heart Of Gold' by Neil Young!

BAR	1.	2.	3.	4.
1.	D Dsus2	Dsus4 D	A Asus2	Asus4 A

Chord Library

Getting Started

Stage 1

Stage 2

Stage 3

Stage 4

Stage 5

Stage 6

Stage 7

Stage 8

Stage 9

Bonus

 Here's a reminder of all the chords we've looked at so far...

D	A	A	E	G	G5
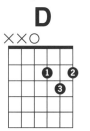	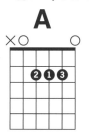	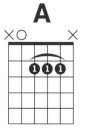	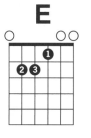	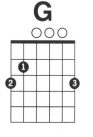	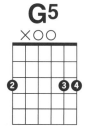

G	G	C	Am	Em	Dm
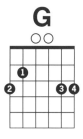	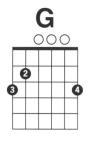	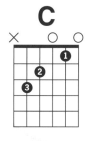	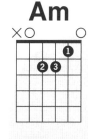		

A7	D7	E7	E7	G7	C7
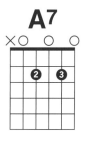	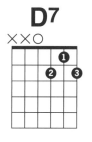	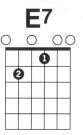		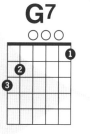	

B7	Asus2	Asus4	Dsus2	Dsus4	Esus4
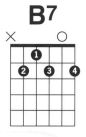		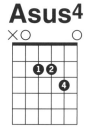	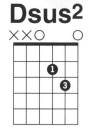	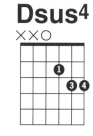	

F	F	F	Fmaj7	Fmaj7	D/F#
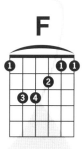	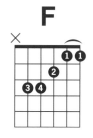	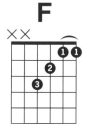	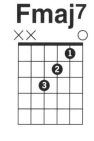	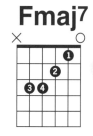	

G/B	C/G	C/G	Cadd9
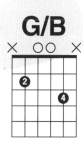	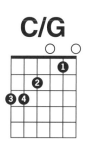	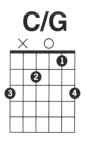	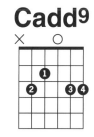

... and here are some more chords to try!

 Minor 7 Chords   CD 2 Track 27-30

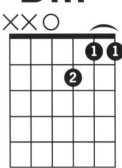 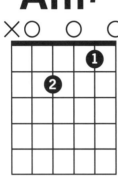 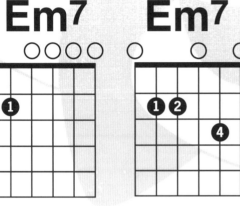

Dm7   **Am7**   **Em7**   **Em7**

 More sus chords   CD 2 Track 31-35

Fsus4   **Fsus2**   **Csus4**   **Csus2**

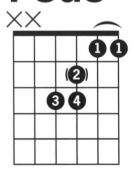 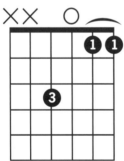 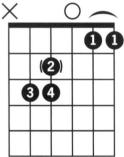 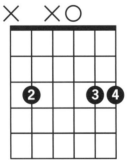

Gsus4

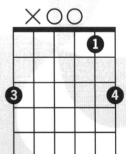

Getting Started | Stage 1 | Stage 2 | Stage 3 | Stage 4 | Stage 5 | Stage 6 | Stage 7 | Stage 8 | Stage 9 | Bonus

Maj7 chords

CD 2 Track 36-39

Amaj7   Dmaj7   Cmaj7   Gmaj7
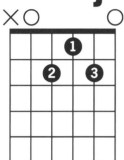 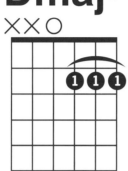 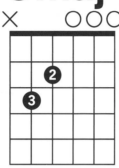 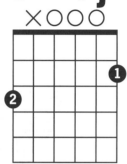

Sus7 chords
CD 2 Track 40-42

D7sus4   A7sus4   E7sus4
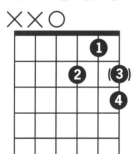 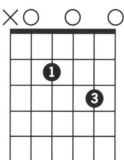 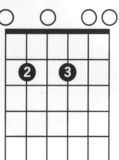

Other cool chords!
CD 2 Track 43-44

Gadd9   Fadd9
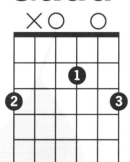 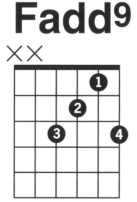

179

Getting
Started

Stage 1

Stage 2

Stage 3

Stage 4

Stage 5

Stage 6

Stage 7

Stage 8

Stage 9

Bonus

 Learning to restring a guitar is a lot easier than you might think, if you do it the right way.

If you can't change your own strings at the moment, and are taking your guitar to the local store to get it done, now is the time to learn. Do be careful though. There is a lot of tension on guitar strings, and if they come loose or snap, they can do you some damage (especially to your eyes).

Also be careful to dispose of your old strings carefully. Cats and dogs really like to chew on them, but they can go straight through their cheeks. So please dispose of them safely (perhaps rolled up and wrapped in paper?).

Remove and replace

Electric Guitars

The first step is to totally remove the original strings. This means taking any bits off the tuning peg, and taking out the 'ball' from the bridge end. There are two main types of electric guitar and two different types of bridge.

On a Fender-type guitar (note: not all Fenders, but most, and also many other brands) the string goes through the guitar and comes out of the back of the guitar. You must check that the ball has been removed from here. If you do not you might get two that wedge themselves in there and it is a real task to get them out. You can check by holding the guitar up to the light and you should be able to see if the ball is still there. If you have any difficulties getting it out then try using the new fat sixth string to poke it out from the front of the guitar. You might also like to try removing the plastic back plate to make it easier to see what you are doing. I leave my back plate off my Strats all the time to make string changing a load quicker.

On a Gibson type guitar (note again that this doesn't apply to all Gibsons) the balls are just hooked through the bridge. You can see these quite easily and should be able to remove them without any problem. Once this has been done you feed the string into the hole where the ball was. On Gibson guitars this means just poking it through the hole toward the neck (sharp end first) and pulling it through until stopped by the ball. On Fender types you must put the string (sharp end first) into the appropriate hole in the back of the guitar (under the plastic rear plate), push it through, grab it at the front and pull it all the way through until stopped by the ball.

Acoustic Guitars

Steel string acoustic guitars have a quite different way of attaching the strings at the bridge end. They rely on a plastic pin to secure the string in place. Again the first step is to remove all of the original strings. Just pull off any remnants from the tuning peg (I usually use long-nose pliers so I don't poke the string into my fingers).

The ball on most steel string acoustics will just fall into the body of the guitar when you break a string, and can be removed by shaking the guitar about until it falls out of the sound hole (this can sometimes prove quite difficult, but is not that important if the ball rattles around inside). You might also like to watch my stupid video about getting a pick out of an acoustic guitar (TB-019)! Next remove the appropriate peg from the bridge. Then put the ball end of the string 10cm into the hole and replace the peg. Then slowly pull the string while keeping some pressure on the peg until the string is tight. Although this may look a little insecure, if done correctly it will be very strong. Watch out if the peg seems to be coming out, just keep pushing it in (quite hard). Once pulled tight it should not have any give.

Getting Started

Stage 1

Stage 2

Stage 3

Stage 4

Stage 5

Stage 6

Stage 7

Stage 8

Stage 9

Bonus

 # Winding on the peg

This part is the same for all types of guitars (except classical guitars). The most important part of this is getting the string on the right side of the peg, and here is how to do it. First of all line up the hole in the peg so it is facing straight down the neck. Put the string through the hole and pull it back so you have some slack. The amount of slack you need will vary, depending on the thickness of the string. The sixth string only needs about 4cm but the first string can take 10cm, or thereabouts. Now hold the string in place with your right hand, just hold the peg so the string cannot slip and then turn the peg ANTI-CLOCKWISE (if you are looking at the peg; if the peg is underneath, like on some Gibson guitars , then it looks clockwise from above).

As you continue turning the peg the string will wrap around it. The first time round the string should go above the hole (and the slack poking out) and above the string, and after one lap it should fall under the string. This will make it lock onto the string as it gets tighter (it is O.K. for all the wraps to go under, but it is just more secure if you get the lock). You should aim for a least two wraps on the sixth string and five wraps for the first string. More will not hurt, but less and the string may start to slip. Try not to let the string overlap itself, as this may make it easier to break.

 # Tuning Up

Tune the strings using any of the methods described on pages 32-33.

Stretching in

The last stage—quite often forgotten—is to stretch the string in. Just gently pull on the string with one hand, using the other hand to hold the string in its correct position in the nut. You should notice it going out of tune considerably, and will need to tune it again. Continue stretching until you no longer need to tune it up.

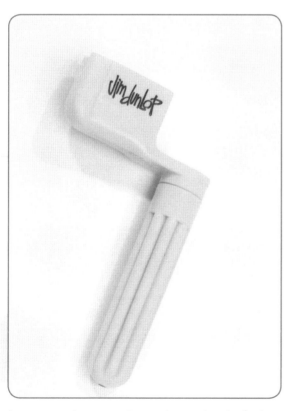

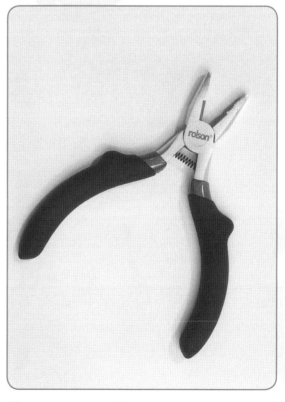

buying a string winder and a good set of pliers will make changing strings much easier.

Getting A Good Sound From Your Amp

Getting
Started

Stage 1

Stage 2

Stage 3

Stage 4

Stage 5

Stage 6

Stage 7

Stage 8

Stage 9

Bonus

 ## Making yourself sound good!

If you bought an electric guitar you might well be struggling with getting a good sound from your amp, so I thought I would run through the basics with you. Of course there are many different types of amplifiers and with all the new-fangled technology found in modelling amps there are even more settings to adjust then ever!

There are two main types of guitar amplifier, Valve and Solid State (also called transistor). Valve amps usually sound better, warmer and clearer, but are heavier and more fragile and generally more expensive. The valves get very, very hot, so be careful if you have to go near them. Never move a hot valve amp or you might damage the valves. However, they are the business and most serious guitarist use valve amps. Solid State amps are more consistent (you don't have to wait for your valves to warm up) and they are easier to control and a lot more reliable than valve models. Some amps have a mix of both valves and transistor technology, some of which sound very good. The newest breed of amplifiers are 'modelling' amps, which are amplifiers with lots of available sounds that are digitally modelled on great amps. These can be a good choice for beginners that want to experiment with different sounds.

Here's an example of a Fender valve amp...

...and here's the very popular Line 6 'Spider' modelling amp.

justinguitar.com

Getting Started

Stage 1

Stage 2

Stage 3

Stage 4

Stage 5

Stage 6

Stage 7

Stage 8

Stage 9

Whatever amp you have, it should have all, or most of these basic settings:

Treble

This is the amount of high end in the sound. High settings of this will make the sound very sharp and crisp. It will make finger and string noise louder and make it scratchier. It's usually set around 5–6; be careful with higher settings as it can make the sound too harsh.

Middle

This is an important control. Middle (mids) settings can change the whole character of the sound. With distortion, taking the mids out (a low setting of 2–3) will give quite a rock sound (called a 'scooped' mid). A higher mid setting on a clean sound will make it more 'honky'. Be careful with the mids. Try a setting around between 3–4, it is unusual to have it set higher than 5–6.

Bass

Usually set around 6-7 or more, this will add low end or bass sound. On some amps you will need to set this higher or the sound will be thin. On very small amps it is hard to get a lot of bass in the sound because the speakers are too small to make them!

Presence

This often is the frequency range between treble and middle and adds a lot of bite to the sound. Presence can be a little confusing because different manufacturers make the presence knob do different things. You will need to experiment with it and find out if it is boosting or cutting the sound. Most presence controls are active, so they can boost sounds as well as cut them.

Filter / Tone / Contour

Adjusts all of the previous settings in one knob. Usually these change the mid frequency and add bass, but they vary. Get to know each unit that uses these controls and experiment to find out what they do.

Gain (distortion)

This controls how much crunch or distortion you will get from your amp. For a clean sound you want to set this as low as possible (off, or 1–2), for a blues sound you might want a little crunch, so a setting of 4–6 would be good, and for rock and metal you want to wind it all the way up to 10!

Master Volume

Some amps have a 'Master' volume which acts as a overall volume control but can also be used to get crunch if there is a regular volume too. To keep it clean, set the Master Volume high (about 8) and then keep the Volume low (3–4). To get some crunch then set the volume high (about 8) and the Master Volume to 3–4. This kind of thing works very differently on different amps so you will have to experiment.

Reverb

This is a kind of short echo, which happens naturally in rooms, but usually not enough to notice in a small room, so by adding it artificially it will make your sound bigger. Be careful about adding too much; a little can really make your sound more pro. Turn it up to 10 and you will soon find out what reverb sounds like!

Because all guitar and amplifiers are different it is very hard for me to be any more exact about what setting your should set your amp to. Different guitars will likely need very different settings and so you have to use your ears. It is important to experiment and play about with the extreme settings of each knob so that you fully understand what it does.

After a while you will get a feel for it and be able to set your amp to whatever sound you desire!

All the notes!

You might find this chart useful if you want to find the notes on the neck, and learning them all is something covered in my book Practical Music Theory.

You should make sure that you know all the notes on the bottom two strings at least because you will use them for your Power Chords and Scale root notes and in the future for your Barre Chords.

If you know the notes on the thickest two strings and you learned all your open position notes when we learned them, then you don't have too many more to learn!

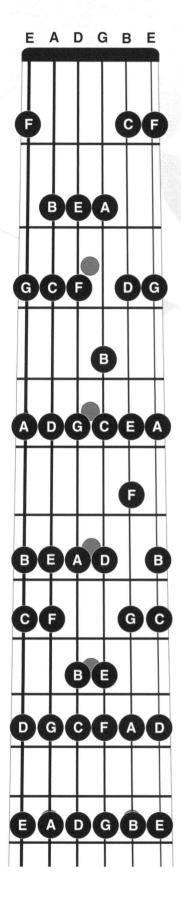

Capo Chart

Introduction

The most common use for a capo is to change the key of a song to fit your voice without having to change the chord shapes. Most songs sung by men will fit a woman's voice better with a capo up four frets, and for a man to sing a female vocal you need to go down (or up) 6 frets. These are just very rough guides of course, because everybody's voice is different, and we all have different ranges where we feel comfortable.

The other main use for a capo is to avoid using difficult barre chords. We can use a capo chart to show the open chords and what chord they become with the capo on each fret. You will probably only have to make the chart once, because once you have done it you will understand it all and not have to use it! And if you have to reference it once in a while, that is O.K. Like everything else, however, you have to try and get all this info into your memory! We've started you off with the first chord shape—A—and given you a few more clues; then you're on your own!

		Capo Fret									
	Open	1	2	3	4	5	6	7	8	9	10
	A	A♯/B♭	B	C	C♯/B♭	D	D♯/E♭	E	F	F♯/G♭	G
	C		D	D♯/E♭		F	F♯/G♭				
	D	E♭/D♯							B♭		
	E			G			A♯/B♭	B			
	G	G♯/A♭	A			C				E	
	Am		Bm				D♯m/E♭m	Em			
	Dm							Am			
	Em		F♯m/G♭m							C♯m	
	Fmaj7				Amaj7	A♯maj7/B♭maj7					

(left side vertical label: OPEN CHORD)

Getting Started

Stage 1

Stage 2

Stage 3

Stage 4

Stage 5

Stage 6

Stage 7

Stage 8

Stage 9

Bonus

 Single Note Recognition (SNR)

As a little introduction to single note playing in this J.U.S.T.I.N. exercise we are going to look at some single notes. Most people find them easier to identify than chords! And, when you get good at this, you can start trying to work out lead guitar solos on your own, which is way cool!

I will only be playing the notes from the A minor pentatonic that you have already learned in the course, so the most important thing here is to pause after you hear the note... play through the notes in the scale and see if you can figure out which one I played.

Before you even start guessing the note I play, try and develop your 'feel' for it by noticing if the note sounds high or low (thin strings or thick string) and the texture of the note if you can... really try and listen deeply and then try and find that note and write it in by showing where the note is on the neck in TAB.

CD 2 Track **45**

Note Palette: A minor pentatonic scale

	Attempt 1	Attempt 2	Attempt 3
1.			
2.			
3.			
4.			
5.			
6.			
7.			
8.			
9.			
10.			

NOTE

There's answers for this on page 192.

A Blues Lead To Learn

Getting Started

Stage 1

Stage 2

Stage 3

Stage 4

Stage 5

Stage 6

Stage 7

Stage 8

Stage 9

Bonus

Introduction

As a starting point for getting into playing lead guitar, I thought you might find it helpful if I wrote out a 12-Bar lead solo for you to experiment with. On CD2 I play it over the backing for the Classic 12-Bar blues shuffle riff, which you should have learned earlier; and then over a professionally recorded backing track. This is included on CD2 on track 48 for you to solo over.

If you have a jam buddy, a really fun thing to do would be to take turns doing the lead solo while the other plays the backing, or you could record yourself playing the 12-Bar backing and then play the lead over it.

The fingering you use for all the notes will be the same as you have been using to practise the A minor pentatonic scale. Don't worry about what picking to use at this stage—do whatever feels comfortable.

Rhythmically the solo is fairly simple; a mixture of quarter notes (notes that last a whole beat), eighth notes (those where there are two notes played in the beat) and some triplets toward the end (where there are three notes played in the beat). I'm expecting you will learn the rhythm by listening, but if you can figure out the count (which notes are played on the beat, and which on the 'ands') then you will find it a great help.

Remember though that this is just a starting point—something to get you going—really, what you want to do is use it as a springboard for your own improvisation. I hope you enjoy it!

CD 2 Track 46-48

Simple Finger Picking: 'Silent Night'

Getting Started

Stage 1

Stage 2

Stage 3

Stage 4

Stage 5

Stage 6

Stage 7

Stage 8

Stage 9

Bonus

 ## Introduction

Christmas is a great time to show off your new skills and this easy Christmas song is lots of fun to play. It will help you develop your fingerstyle playing and give you a go at playing chords and melody together (which is easy for piano players, but hard for us guitar players!). Take this one slowly—there's no rush with it—just take it slow and let your skills develop. If you are new to guitar, this song also makes a great goal to be able to play within a year. If you can do all the stuff in the book and play this song, then you know you are doing really well! For the recording I used an acoustic guitar, but this works equally well on electric. On the CD I play it twice; first slowly and then up to speed.

 ## Bar-by-bar

Bar 1: Use your 2nd and 3rd fingers. Your thumb plays bass and fingers 1, 2 and 3 pluck the second, third and fourth strings. The right hand fingers are nearly always plucking as a group to play the chords.

Bar 2: Just lift off the 3rd finger.

Bar 5: Use 1st finger barré at 5th fret.

Bar 6: A standard D chord.

Bar 7: Use 1st finger on second string, 2nd finger on first string, and 3rd finger on the third string.

Bar 9: Standard C chord.

Bar 10: Lift off the 3rd finger and add your little finger on thinnest string. The third finger will naturally fall in place to play the F# note (2nd fret) on its own. Make sure you note that the bass string is now the fourth string.

Bar 11: This is like the intro, only without the bass note.

Bar 13: Use 1st finger barré at the 5th fret.

Bar 14: Move barré up two frets and add 2nd finger on the thinnest string. Hold down the chord while the little finger plays the melody note and then lifts off.

Bar 16: Just like a D chord, but up at the 7th fret.

Bar 17: Use 3rd finger on the thinnest string and hold down the chord while you use the 2nd finger to play the next melody note and the open second string.

Bar 18: Use 2nd finger on the thickest string, 3rd finger on the third string and your little finger on the second string. Then lift off your little finger and have your 1st finger ready in the 1st fret. Leave the rest of the chord down the whole time and just pluck out the melody note on the third string.

Bar 20: Use harmonics at the 12th fret. Touch the strings very lightly right above the fret, not just behind, where you might normally.

I hope you like it! Leave any questions in the Forum at www.justinguitar. com. Once you have this basic arrangement mastered, try playing around with the rhythms and the chords and see if you can come up with something special that is your own.

Getting Started

Stage 1

Stage 2

Stage 3

Stage 4

Stage 5

Stage 6

Stage 7

Stage 8

Stage 9

Bonus

Getting Started

Stage 1

Stage 2

Stage 3

Stage 4

Stage 5

Stage 6

Stage 7

Stage 8

Stage 9

Bonus

Introduction

Many people like playing solo blues guitar and this song was so popular on YouTube that I wrote a series of solo blues pieces which are available on DVD. This one is aimed at beginners and is mixing together lead and rhythm. You can see that it is using the 'Chunka Chunka' blues style and mixes it up with some lead guitar lines.

The cool thing about this type of song is that it doesn't really need any accompaniment and sounds complete when you play it on its own. As your playing develops you can also explore improvising in the lead and rhythm guitar sections which makes it lots of fun and very interesting! Again, for the recording I used an acoustic guitar, and play it twice on the CD at two different speeds.

Bar-by-bar

Bars 1–2: This is a classic blues intro. In the first bar use your 3rd finger on the third string and your little finger on the thinnest string. In the second bar, use your 1st finger on the 1st fret of the third string for the first mini E chord and then use your 1st finger for the climb up to the full B7 chord. Notice that this riff starts on beat 2.

Bars 3–4: This is the classic 12-Bar Blues Shuffle Riff in action! Your 2nd finger will play the one note that is in the 3rd fret, otherwise it's all using first and 3rd fingers!

Bars 5–6: After playing a small open E power chord, we move into a lead line using the E minor pentatonic. In bar 5, use your 3rd finger for the notes in the 3rd fret, and your 2nd finger for notes in the 2nd fret. In bar 6, play the first note with your 1st finger, and then use your 3rd and 4th fingers—like you did in the intro—for the next two pairs of notes, shifting the same grip up a fret. Hold the two notes in the 4th fret down and let them ring out while you play the note on the thickest string, 3rd fret with your first finger!

Bar 7: Another bar of the 12-Bar shuffle riff

Bar 8: A bar of lead using the E Minor Pentatonic. Start with the little chord (1st finger only), and then move into the lead line, using your 3rd finger in the 3rd fret and 2nd finger for notes in 2nd fret as before.

Bar 9: One of the 12-Bar shuffle riff variations!

Bar 10: A little riff in E, all these notes should be played with your first finger!

Bar 11: Regular B7 chord… put your 2nd finger down first for the root note and then get the rest of the chord down as quick as you can.

Bar 12: A chord, and then another E minor pentatonic lick… use your 3rd finger for notes in the 3rd fret, and 2nd finger for notes in the 2nd fret.

Bar 13: This is a 'turnaround' lick. A chord first, then use the same finger as the fret number!

Bar 14: Open strings, then use 1st finger for the note on 1st fret and get to the B7 Chord. Note the 1st Time bar and the repeat sign. This means that the first time you come to this point you play it, and then when you hit the repeat sign you go back the earlier repeat sign at the start of bar 3, and play from there again; only this time, when you get to the 1st time bar you ain't allowed in: you have to go the 2nd time bar. Get it?

Bar 15: The Little ending lick is here in the 2nd time Bar. Play open strings, then use whatever fingers you like for the two notes in the 2nd fret, finishing with an E7 chord (the type that has a note D on the second string).

Once you have this mastered, try playing around with the lead breaks—which all use the E minor pentatonic—and see if you can come up with your own blues licks in those bars.

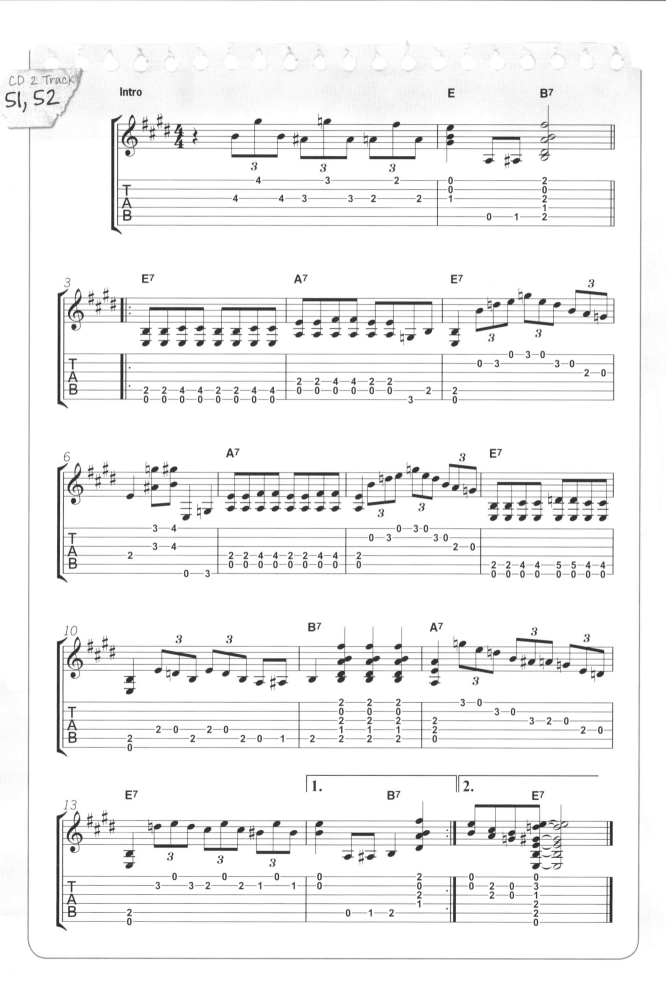

justinguitar.com

Getting Started

Stage 1

Stage 2

Stage 3

Stage 4

Stage 5

Stage 6

Stage 7

Stage 8

Stage 9

Bonus

CD 2 Track
51, 52

Getting Started

Stage 1

Stage 2

Stage 3

Stage 4

Stage 5

Stage 6

Stage 7

Stage 8

Stage 9

Bonus

CD 1

1	BC-109	Tuning Notes
2	BC-111	D Chord
3	BC-112	A Chord
4	BC-113	E Chord
5	BC-116	Four-To-The-Bar Strumming
6	BC-118	J.U.S.T.I.N. Introduction
7		J.U.S.T.I.N.-1-2-SSR
8		J.U.S.T.I.N.-1-3-CPR
9	BC-121	Am Chord
10	BC-122	Em Chord
11	BC-123	Dm Chord
12	BC-128	J.U.S.T.I.N.-2-1-CQR
13		J.U.S.T.I.N.-2-1-SSR
14		J.U.S.T.I.N.-2-3-CPR
15	BC-131	G Chord
16	BC-132	C Chord
17	BC-135	Basic Finger Workout
18		Basic Finger Workout (whole exercise)
19	BC-136	RUST 1
20		RUST 2
21		RUST 2: E to A
22	BC-138	J.U.S.T.I.N.-3-1-CQR
23		J.U.S.T.I.N.-3-2-SSR
24		J.U.S.T.I.N.-3-3-CPR
25	BC-141	G7 Chord
26		C7 Chord
27		B7 Chord
28	BC-142	Fmaj7
29	BC-143	A With Mini-Barre
30	BC-146	RUST 4
31		RUST 8
32	BC-148	J.U.S.T.I.N.-4-1-CQR
33		J.U.S.T.I.N.-4-2-SSR
34		J.U.S.T.I.N.-4-3-CPR
35	BC-151	A7 Chord
36		D7 Chord
37		E7 Chord
38		E7 Chord with high D
39	BC-155	Triplet Rhythm
40	BC-156	Shuffle Rhythm
41	BC-158	J.U.S.T.I.N.-5-1-CQR
42		J.U.S.T.I.N.-5-2-SSR
43		J.U.S.T.I.N.-5-3-CPR
44	BC-161	F Chord Version #1 (Full Barre)
45		F Chord Version #2
46		F Chord Version #3
47	BC-165	RUST 9
48	BC-166	Picking Exercises 1 - 4
49	BC-168	J.U.S.T.I.N.-6-1-CQR
50		J.U.S.T.I.N.-6-2-SSR
51		J.U.S.T.I.N.-6-3-CPR
52	BC-172	G5 Power Chord
53	BC-173	Asus4 Chord
54		Asus2 Chord
55		Dsus4 Chord
56		Dsus2 Chord
57		Esus4 Chord
58	BC-175	RUST 16
59	BC-176	The A Minor Pentatonic Scale
60	BC-178	J.U.S.T.I.N.-7-1-CQR
61		J.U.S.T.I.N.-7-2-SSR
62		J.U.S.T.I.N.-7-3-CPR

CD 2

1	BC-181	'Big' G Chord
2		'Rock' G Chord
3		'Folk' G Chord
4		Cadd9
5	BC-183	12-Bar Blues Shuffle Riff
6	BC-184	Basic Fingerstyle
7	BC-186	C5 Power Chord
8	BC-188	J.U.S.T.I.N.-8-1-CQR
9		J.U.S.T.I.N.-8-2-SSR
10		J.U.S.T.I.N.-8-3-CPR
11	BC-191	D/F♯ Chord
12		G/B Chord
13		C/G Chord Version #1
14		C/G Chord Version #2
15	BC-192	Palm Muting
16	BC-193	Fingerstyle Patterns
17	BC-194	12-Bar Blues Variations
18		12-Bar blues Variations #1
19		12-Bar Blues Variations #2
20		12-Bar Blues Variations #3
21		12-Bar Blues Variations #4
22	BC-195	Minor Pentatonic Patterns #1
23		Minor Pentatonic Patterns #2
24	BC-198	J.U.S.T.I.N.-9-1-CQR
25		J.U.S.T.I.N.-9-2-SSR
26		J.U.S.T.I.N.-9-3-CPR
27	BC-201	Dm7 Chord
28		Am7 Chord
29		Em7 Chord Version #1
30		Em7 Chord Version #2
31		Fsus4 Chord
32		Fsus2 Chord
33		Csus4 Chord
34		Csus2 Chord
35		Gsus4 Chord
36		Amaj7 Chord
37		Dmaj7 Chord
38		Cmaj7 Chord
39		Gmaj7 Chord
40		D7sus4 Chord
41		A7sus4 Chord
42		E7sus4 Chord
43		Gadd9 Chord
44		Fadd9 Chord
45	BC-206	J.U.S.T.I.N. – BONUS – SNR
46	BC-207	Blues Lead (Shuffle Riff Backing)
47		Blues Lead (Full Demo)
48		Blues Lead (Backing Track Only)
49	BC-208	'Silent Night' (Slow)
50		'Silent Night' (Fast)
51	BC-209	Solo Blues (Slow)
52		Solo Blues (Fast)

SINGLE NOTE RECOGNITION

J.U.S.T.I.N. TEST ANSWERS FOR BONUS STAGE

THE ANSWERS! NO PEEKING...

1) Third String, 5th fret
2) First String, 5th fret
3) Third String, 7th fret
4) Fifth String, 7th fret
5) Second String, 8th fret
6) First String, 8th fret
7) Sixth String, 5th fret
8) Fifth String, 5th fret
9) Second String, 5th fret
10) Fourth String, 7th fret

123456789